D0875999

BEHIND THAT WALL

By the same author

MOTHER OF CARMEL: A Portrait of St. Teresa of Jesus
SPIRIT OF FLAME: A Study of St. John of the Cross
FOOL OF LOVE: The Life of Ramon Lull

BEHIND THAT WALL

AN INTRODUCTION TO SOME
CLASSICS OF THE INTERIOR LIFE

E. ALLISON PEERS

My Beloved . . . standeth behind our wall
CANTICLES 2:9

MOREHOUSE-GORHAM CO., NEW YORK

PRINTED IN THE UNITED STATES OF AMERICA BY
THE HADDON CRAFTSMEN, INC., SCRANTON, PA.

TO

ERIC FAIRFAX ROBSON

A small tribute of great affection

PREFACE

NEARLY all the essays in this book have been broadcast in the Home or the Latin-American service of the B.B.C. and are being published at the request of many listeners; the remainder have been given at various times as sermons or addresses. They are thus essentially talks, rather than readings, and, in recasting them, I have retouched them very little, retaining many phrases suggestive of personal contact. They are intended, of course, to serve as introductions to the study of the books they describe, and my chief hope, in publishing them, is that they will send many to the originals, about which, in the restricted space at my disposal, I have been able to say so little.

The notes on editions and studies to be found at the end of each essay have purposely been kept as short as possible, lest the interested but unlearned reader should find them bewildering. It must not for a moment be assumed that, because any particular work is omitted, it is not recommended. The editions from which quotations have been made are indicated by an asterisk.

E.A.P.

CONTENTS

INTRODUCTION

Behind that Wall

INTRODUCTION

Behind that Wall

IN THAT beautiful love-poem, the Song of Solomon, a poem full of pictures, there is one picture which I discovered a long time ago and which made a very deep impression on me: "My Beloved . . . standeth behind our wall."

"Behind our wall." A wall! What an ugly thing! Useful, of course; necessary, of course; but how dull! Almost as dull as my life—or yours. Watch it being built: not of anything attractive, like marble, alabaster or porphyry, but of common, rough, ugly bricks, placed one upon another —brick upon brick, brick upon brick, for yard upon yard. Just like life, you say. Day upon day, day upon day: same morning train, same sordid streets, same dingy office, same dull routine. Or, if you're the person left at home, same crowded shops, same heavy baskets, same cramped house, same annoying neighbours, same dusting, same cooking, same cleaning, same mending—you know it all by heart.

And, you sometimes say, what *does* it all lead to? After you've seen five or ten yards of that wall you can guess what the rest will be like. And after you've lived five or ten years of that life you can see all the rest stretching out before you: when you're young, you think it will never come to an end; when you're old, you don't care how soon it does. You look ahead, ten, twenty, thirty years, and you see yourself, all the time, building that dull wall of your life till you're worn out. You can't escape building it: we're all wall-builders, whether we like it or no. And as a rule you can't build it of more interesting materials. Most lives, to outward appearance, are made up of duties, with a considerable admixture of self-denials and disappointments. Even that imposing wall in the principal thoroughfare of the city, which you gaze at so enviously as you pass it every day, proves, on a closer examination, to be much the same as your own. And that exciting, adventurous-looking one, you ask—the one I was telling you about last Friday? Oh, that! Why, it was so badly built that it collapsed on Saturday morning. Yes, most walls are much the same really. And in any case, it isn't the wall that's important; it's the way you build it. What matters is whether you build it from the outside or from the inside. And, if you build it from the inside, who is behind it with you. Those are the things I want to consider as a preface to these short studies of some lives lived "Behind that wall."

You can't tell much about a wall by taking a look at it from the outside. Two walls anywhere look very much the same. So do two lives. Here, for example, are two people spending all their time at office work, or shopping, or cleaning. If you don't know them well, you can't see any difference between them. And yet, though they may both have the same sized income, one of them is rich and one is poor. One is radiantly happy; the other is eternally discontented. To one, life is full of meaning and purpose; to the other, hollow and empty. One exists on stimulants—an unhealthy diet of excitements and pleasures; the other, silently and imperceptibly, is being fed by a living spring of deep joy. Here are two walls—two lives—to all appearance as dull and unadventurous as can be. But *are* they? No. For behind one of them is—nothing; behind the other—the Beloved.

I remember, years ago, in the south of Spain, living in an old city built on two hills with a valley between them. On one hill stood a great many fine country houses and a famous mediæval castle. On the other, there is little but dirty streets, dilapidated houses and slums.

One day, down in the valley, I met a very pleasant person, who asked me to his house to have tea with him. "I live up there on the hill," he said. "You mean the hill with the castle?" I asked. "No," he said, "the other one." I suppose I must have looked surprised, because he added: "Oh, you'll like my house, I assure you. And it's quite easy to find. Just go straight up that street till you come to a whitewashed wall on the right. Behind that wall is my home."

So the next afternoon I set out to walk up the narrow cobbled street. It was a sweltering day; the road twisted and turned; I stumbled over the loose stones; there was no proper drainage; children screamed in their high-pitched voices; yoked oxen and heavily laden mules drove one to the side of the road. It was as monotonous and unpleasant a walk as I had ever had.

Then, sure enough, on my right hand, there loomed up a tall, endless-looking white wall, and I knew my walk was coming to an end. At last I found a little door in the wall. I opened it and went in. And I saw—well, I can't even begin to describe it.

The air was full of the scent of orange-trees, with their glossy leaves and starry white flowers. There were trellised roses; there were banks of carnations; there were tall, overshadowing acacias. There was a fountain, and a pool flanked by arum lilies. There was a mass of blue wistaria hiding the large house. And out of the house came my host smiling at my look of astonishment. "Not such a bad place to come back to after a day's work in the city!" he said.

Now the lives of many people, to those who don't know them, may seem no more interesting than that white-washed wall. But really they're like that garden. Because behind their wall stands the Beloved. There He is, doing His marvellous work, turning the flint into a fountain of waters, making the desert blossom as the rose. The dull routine takes on a new aspect when He goes through it with you. The trivial duties become privileges when He is by your side. The self-denials and the disappointments still come, but He means so much more than anything else that His presence transforms them. "They looked unto Him," says the Psalmist, "and were lightened"—that is, they were illumined, they became radiant. But they could never have looked unto Him at all if they had not been on His side of the wall.

Very often the life that is lived behind that wall is called the inner, or the interior, life. And I could easily devote the whole of this book, and many more like it, to describing that life in itself. You may need directions, for example, for finding the door in the wall that takes you behind it: not all of us have the strength and the skill, as David had, to leap over it. Then there is the work to be done there: you may have to pull down the parts of the wall you've built from the outside and build it up again from the inside. Again, when you have succeeded in getting behind the wall, how do you find the Beloved? Sometimes, of course, He is waiting there and you see Him at once. Sometimes you just start work and He comes quietly, "without noise of words," and is with you before you know it. Sometimes you can't find Him, and He doesn't come—but let the poet tell us about that:

> It may be that to spy thee He is mounting
> Upon a tower,
> Or in thy counting
> Thou hast mista'en the hour.

But, if He comes not, neither do thou go
  Till Vesper chime.
Belike thou then shalt know
  He hath been with thee all the time.

However, the task I have set myself in these pages is to tell you about some of the great men and women who have lived behind the wall, and about the records they have left us in the shape of books describing their experiences. However difficult we may find it ourselves to live the interior life, however much our work or our troubles may oppress us, however hard it may be to shake off the world and to concentrate on the things that matter most, I think we ought sometimes to read books by people who have been more successful at this than ourselves, even if in places we are unable altogether to understand them.

After all, we are ready enough to look at great pictures, or to listen to great symphonies, though I don't suppose for a moment we understand them all or can get as much out of them as the man who made them put in. And we like looking at them, or listening to them, because we find more in them every time; and also, I think, because we realize how much more there is to be got out of them in the future. We never feel we have taken their full measure or exhausted their possibilities. We know that far beyond our normal span there lies a beauty which the great artists who have created it are trying to pass on to us. Even truer is that of the still greater souls who have experienced Beauty uncreated.

O heavenly Beauty, lovelier far
Than any beauty we can know,
On starriest night thou fairest star,
Thou light most glorious from below,
Thou hidden world with radiant glow!

Whenever I can, I want to stand back and let these great lovers of our Lord Jesus Christ tell us, in their own words, about themselves and about Him. For they are like great painters and great musicians, like explorers who discover new lands or scale high mountains. They can describe to us the things they have seen and experienced behind the wall. They can tell us some of the secrets of their most intimate communion with God. And perhaps they can help us to penetrate a little farther into that golden country of our deep desire, "where Christ is all and in all."

Who are they? What are their names? What are they like? Well, there are far too many of them for me to do more than name a few. There was the Beloved Disciple, who in this life leaned on the Master's breast. There was St. Paul, who saw Him in a vision and came to be so close to Him that he could say: "I live, yet not I, but Christ liveth in me." There was St. Augustine, author of those vivid *Confessions* and of an eloquent book which we shall glance at in these pages—*The City of God*. St. Bernard, whose hymns on the love of Jesus are sung in all our churches. St. Francis of Assisi, who bore in his body the marks of the Lord Jesus. St. Ignatius of Loyola, who founded a sixteenth-century Salvation Army. St. Francis Xavier, who joined that Army and gave up his life to preaching the Gospel in the Far East.

Another thing: they are people of all kinds, of all ages, of all countries—and, what is more important, they are people who have lived all types of life. No one has sung the love of God more sweetly than the Italian Jacopone da Todi, and Jacopone was a lawyer. The Majorcan, Ramon Lull, was a courtier who became a missionary and a great believer in language-teaching. Suso, the German, and Ruysbroeck, the Fleming, were contemplatives in the cloister, and Richard Rolle, the Englishman, was a hermit; but St. Jane Chantal, a Frenchwoman, was a busy housewife, left a widow, at twenty-eight, with four small children. Benjamin Whichcote was a don, a Provost of King's, but Jacob Boehme was a shoemaker. Brother Lawrence practised the presence of God while he worked in the kitchen, and St. Teresa, who spent a great deal of her time cooking and spinning, once declared that "God walks among the pots and pans"—and not only in the Garden of Eden.

Well, those are a few of them, and hardly anyone reading these lives will fail to find someone like himself. Yet, unlike each other as they are, they all lived "behind that wall." And in the pages which follow I want to look at some of the books they have left us.

These, you will find, are as varied as their authors. One of them, *The Imitation of Christ*, was written in the fifteenth century by a Flemish monk for men and women in the cloister but has been read and loved by millions of people living in the world who are hard pressed from morning to night. Another, a sixteenth-century book from Spain—*The Interior Castle*—is the work of one of the most practical women who ever lived. Another, again, is a collection of verse, written, a hundred years later still, by a Welsh doctor, who gave it the curious but rather striking title of *The Flint flashing fire*. There is something here for everyone who loves beauty and longs to have more of it or who feels the need of purpose and inspiration. Read about all these books, then re-read the chapters which appeal to you most; and finally examine the short bibliography at the end of each chapter and make the acquaintance of the books themselves—all, as I say, so unlike, yet all inspired by the same Beauty and the same Truth:

> O heavenly Truth, that here dost shine,
> A beacon-light our path to guide,
> Set by a hand unseen, divine,
> To all revealed, to none denied,
> On high, yet ever at our side!

"Ever at our side!" Behind that wall.

I

ST. AUGUSTINE

The City of God

I

ST. AUGUSTINE

The City of God

THE AUGUSTINE who wrote *The City of God*, and the more famous *Confessions*, must not be confused with the Saint of the same name who was the first Archbishop of Canterbury. The Archbishop was the latter of the two; he was a Roman, and a protégé of St. Gregory the Great, who sent him to convert England: you remember the story of the fair-haired children in the slave market, "not Angles, but Angels." That St. Augustine died about the year 600. But this one—St. Augustine the Great, to give him his full title—was an African, and lived much earlier, from 354 to 430.

Augustine was born near Bone, about one hundred miles west of Bizerta. His father was a pagan, later converted to Christianity; but his mother, Monica, was a Christian—and she has become the accepted type of the praying mother and one of the most famous women in history. At sixteen he went to Carthage, near Tunis, to study law. He was a not uncommon type—all intellect and no moral principles; and instead of becoming a servant of Christ like his mother, he joined the heretical sect of the Manicheans. These were people who had a highbrow kind of religion: the Bible, they said, was full of foolish fables; and man, having no free will, was unable to help sinning—in fact, he was tossed to and fro all the time between two eternal principles, good and evil. Augustine thought these ideas very attractive, especially the part about not being able to help sinning, until he began to examine them, and then he saw through them and was too honest to profess them any more. Still, he loved his sins; and, though he knew he would have to give them up some day, he used to pray a prayer which has become famous: "O God, give me chastity—but not yet." "I was afraid," he confessed later, "that God would hear me soon."

Not till he was thirty-three did he yield. He had gone to Italy—to Milan—as professor; he had been joined there by his mother; he had begun to study Christian doctrine. And then suddenly came his conversion. Let him tell that story himself—how he

> heard from a neighbouring house a voice, as of boy or girl, I know not, chanting, and oft repeating, "Take up and read. Take up and read." Instantly, my countenance altered, I began to think most intently, whether children were wont in any kind of play to sing such words: nor could I remember ever to have heard the like . . . I arose; interpreting it to be no other than a command from God, to open the book, and read the first chapter I should find . . . I seized, opened, and in silence read that section on which my eyes first fell: "Not in rioting and drunkenness, not in chambering and wantonness, not in strife and envying; but

> put ye on the Lord Jesus Christ, and make not provision for the flesh, in concupiscence." No further would I read; nor needed I: for instantly at the end of this sentence, by a light as it were of serenity infused into my heart, all the darkness of doubt vanished away.

That was St. Augustine's conversion. No dazzling light, no mysterious voice, no sudden blindness, as with St. Paul. Just a mother's prayers, a Bible and the voice of a child at play.

So he was baptized. And in time he was ordained. And at forty-two he became Bishop of Hippo, a city near his birthplace. That bishopric he held for thirty-four years, until his death at the age of seventy-six. There he founded the Augustinian Order, of men who tried to live like the first disciples, with everything in common, and he made his bishop's palace a residence for clergy of the Order, all of them vowed to poverty.

To-day his best-known book is the *Confessions*, one of the most remarkable autobiographies in the world. The word *Confessions* here does not mean expressions of repentance, though of course he does say a good deal about the bad years of his life, for which he is full of contrition. What he chiefly confesses is the glory of God:

> What do I love, when I love Thee? Not beauty of bodies, nor the fair harmony of time, nor the brightness of the light, so gladsome to our eyes, nor sweet melodies of varied songs, nor the fragrant smell of flowers, and ointments, and spices, not manna and honey, not limbs acceptable to

> embracements of flesh. None of these I love, when I love my God; and yet I love a kind of light, and melody, and fragrance, and meat, and embracement, when I love my God, the light, melody, fragrance, meat, embracement of my inner man: where there shineth unto my soul what space cannot contain, and there soundeth what time beareth not away, . . . This is it which I love, when I love my God.

In lyric passages like these he writes canticles and meditations far lovelier than the modern hymn. His book is a legacy to Christians of every age.

But Augustine's principle aim as a writer was to combat heresy and uphold the Christian faith. He had been so much deceived himself that he had a passionate desire to help others. A great part of his later life is the story of his strife with the Donatists and the Pelagians, and it was in the midst of a struggle against Arianism that he died.

The City of God is a book which we owe to a great disaster. In the year 410 Rome had been attacked and captured by the Goths. It is very hard for us to imagine what a terrible shock that was. You may perhaps remember how we felt, in 1940, when we heard that the Germans had entered Paris—a city which we had somehow imagined was certain to hold out, whatever else happened. After that the place in the world which people who loved freedom pinned their faith to was London. Now try to imagine what the shock would have been—not just to us, but all over the world—if one day in the autumn of 1940 London had fallen, too. People would have felt that, in spite of all their prayers and beliefs and hopes, wrong had triumphed over right, and nothing could stop the aggressor now from enslaving the whole world.

Things were rather like that when Rome fell. Once, for many centuries, that city had been the prosperous centre of a pagan Empire. Then the Emperor had become a Christian and for just upon a hundred years Rome had been thought of as the centre of a triumphant Christendom. And now Alaric the Goth had overthrown it. When it had been a pagan city, it had gone from victory to victory and reigned supreme; now, as a Christian city, it had been over-run—it had fallen. You see what inference unsympathetic critics would draw from the contrast between the pagan and the Christian Rome: Christianity, they would say, was done for; the future lay with the pagan gods.

And it was that disaster which produced *The City of God*. Now this is neither a short book nor an easy one, and it would take a great many pages to give an adequate description of it. It has twenty-two parts, and, in any unabridged edition, well over one thousand pages. Sometimes, I think, its magnitude rather obscures its greatness.

Again, its plan is not too clear. Years and years went to its writing; it would be laid down, and, after long intervals, taken up again; it has digressions and discursive arguments which perplex the ordinary reader.

Then, too, it is encyclopædic in range—it can be read for its theology, its philosophy, its history, its apologetics, its ethics, its political theory—or for the picture it gives of its author.

How shall we read a book like that? Students, of course, will look at it differently, but these chapters are not for students: they are for ordinary people who enjoy reading books. And what I would suggest to you about *The City of God* is this. Don't try to read it through, at any rate at the beginning. Pick it up and dip into it here and there. Gather honey from it as the bees gather honey from the flowers in the garden. I can tell you here only a few of the things that are found in it: there are, of course, a great many others.

The first thing that strikes one is the basic conception of the "two cities." Neither of them is intended to represent any kind of visible, organized community. They symbolize people who live by the laws of God and people who live by the standards of man. Where your love is, says St. Augustine, there is your city. Love of self, even to contempt of God, leads us to the earthly city; love of God, even to contempt of self, to the heavenly city. That emphatic contrast, which must have seemed a kind of challenge to a temporarily victorious enemy, has a further meaning for us to-day. For these are realistic days, when we are impatient with people who gloss and blur unpleasant truths, when we want above all to know things as they are. The realism of *The City of God* will send us back to the realism of the New Testament, where we are continually reminded that there are *two* sides, *two* camps, *two* masters, *two* futures, and that each of us has to choose between them. When disaster overtakes our ideals, it should only make us, as it made St. Augustine, more eager to sharpen the distinction and clarify the issue; perhaps that is the surest test of our citizenship.

Then there is St. Augustine's detailed picture of the City of God, to which he returned again and again with such evident delight. It is inhabited, like the Holy City of the Revelation, by "all nations and kindreds and people and tongues," and it "increases itself out of all languages." So comprehensive and so broad it is, so high above all intolerance and pettiness! "It is nothing to the City of God," St. Augustine says, "what attire the citizens wear, or what rules they observe, so long as they contradict not God's holy precepts, but each one keeps the faith, the true path to salvation." Or again, speaking of the contemplative and the active life, "One may not be so much given to contemplation as to neglect the good of his neighbour, nor so much in love with action as to forget Divine speculation." And from this broad and firm earthly foundation St. Augustine's building soars magnificently until it reaches Heaven,

> where there shall be no evil thing, where no good thing shall lie hidden, and where we shall have leisure to utter forth the praises of God, which shall be all things in all.

Hear the dignified movement of the language in the final chapter:

This seventh day shall be our Sabbath, the end whereof shall not be the evening, but the Day of the Lord, like to the eighth eternal day, sanctified and hallowed by the resurrection of Christ, a token of eternal rest, alike of spirit and of body. There shall we rest and see; there, see and love; and there love and praise. Behold what shall be in the end without end! For what other thing is our end save to attain to that kingdom which is without end?

As we read this book, the shadows of the world fall away from us and the outlines of the City become more real. And once immersed in its atmosphere, we find that there are many things of which St. Augustine writes with great beauty, which we can appreciate as we have never done before. One of these is peace, which (he says) "all men do love" and "they that live not according to faith angle for in the sea of temporal profit," but only the citizens of the City of God can obtain. None of the finest of these passages will yield up its full truth or beauty at a first reading, but one of them perhaps will inspire the search for more:

Peace of body is the well-ordered disposal of the parts thereof. Peace of the unreasonable soul is the well-ordered rest of its appetites. Peace of the reasonable soul is a well-ordered harmony between knowledge and conduct. Peace of body and soul alike is the well-ordered life and good estate of the entire creature. Peace of mortal man with immortal God is well-ordered obedience, performed in faith, unto His eternal law. Peace of man with man is a well-ordered concord. Peace of a family is a well-ordered concord between its members as touching rule and obedience. Peace of a city, the well-ordered concord of the citizens. . . . Peace of the City of God, a well-ordered concord in God, for the enjoyment of God.

Peace, in time of war; serenity, in days of turmoil; security and confidence amid doubt, misgiving and unrest.

In vain the surge's angry shock,
  In vain the drifting sands:
Unharmed upon the eternal Rock
  The Eternal City stands.

That is the dominant note of St. Augustine's book. When was such a book more needed?

"Glorious things are spoken of thee, O City of God."

BOOKS

EDITIONS

* *The City of God*. Trans. JOHN HEALEY. London, 1931. (Three volumes as one.)

Confessions. There are numerous editions of the *Confessions*. That used in the text above is Pusey's translation, reprinted in the Red Letter Library, London, 1903.

STUDIES

St. Augustine's *City of God*. J. RICKABY. London, 1925.

II

ST. BERNARD

The Book of the Love of God

II

ST. BERNARD

The Book of the Love of God

St. Bernard of Clairvaux, like St. Augustine the Great, is the victim of a widespread misconception. The only thing that many people know about St. Augustine is that he was the first Archbishop of Canterbury—which he was not. And the only thing that many people know about St. Bernard is that he wrote the popular hymn "Jerusalem the Golden"—which he did not. The author of that hymn, and of a number of others —"For thee, O dear, dear country," "Brief life is here our portion," "The world is very evil," all translated by John Mason Neale—was another man of the same name, a certain Bernard of Cluny, about whom nothing is known except that he lived at about the same time as our Bernard, and, like him, was a Benedictine. Our Bernard did write a famous hymn, "Jesu, dulcis memoria," also translated by Neale, as "Jesu, the very thought is sweet," and by a no less industrious translator, Edward Caswall, in a version better known, but, I think, distinctly inferior:

> Jesu, the very thought of Thee
> With sweetness fills my breast;

But sweeter far Thy face to see
And in Thy presence rest.

St. Bernard's life covers approximately the first half of the twelfth century. His parents were Burgundian aristocrats, who gave him a good humanistic education. As a child, he absorbed a great deal of poetry, and was particularly attached to some of the finest poetry in the world—the poetical books of the Bible. At one time, indeed, he hoped to make the study of the Bible his lifework.

However, in the providence of God, he became an organizer rather than a student. In 1098, about twelve miles from Dijon, his birthplace, there was founded the celebrated monastery of Cisteaux, or Cîteaux, by some people who called themselves Cistercians, who wanted to restore the rule of St. Benedict in its primitive form. When Bernard was twenty-two, he gathered around him a group of his aristocratic friends intent on the religious life, and, after a preparatory period of six months, they went to Cîteaux and begged for admission. Stern and austere though the life was, Bernard took to it immediately, and, at the end of only two years, he was sent to found a new house near by.

The name of that house has become indissolubly associated with his own. The site was not attractive—"a place of horror and vast solitude," an old writer terms it. Though on the bank of a river, it was barren, and on either side were steep hills, covered with dark and gloomy trees. It was called "Valley of bitterness." But Bernard soon found a better name for it. The valley opened towards the southeast and each summer morning it was flooded with sunlight. Bernard used to feel that those gloriously bright hours were an inspiration for the whole day. "Don't call it Valley of Bitterness," he said. "Call it Bright Valley—Claire Vallée, or Clair Vaux."

(Before we go on, isn't it worth while thinking over that story for a moment? I dare say there are many valleys of bitterness in our lives which the sun will flood with light every morning if we will open the windows of our soul and let it in. Often, I am sure, the mere naming of some trouble "Bright Valley" will begin the work of transformation. At any rate, we might try.)

The life at Clairvaux, as at Cîteaux, was very strict and severe—"plain living and high thinking" at a time when people in St. Bernard's station of life thought very little and ate a great deal. The monks took only one meal a day and touched neither fish, nor meat, nor eggs, nor white bread, even at the great festivals. "To an idler," wrote St. Bernard, "cabbage, beans and coarse bread are distasteful, but to one who works hard they are delicacies."

At the age of thirty, St. Bernard, now recognized as a man of unusual prudence and power, was consecrated Abbot of Clairvaux. Soon after this his public life began. There was a schism in the papacy. Two men were elected to the See of Peter, and one of them banished the other, who took refuge in France. The French bishops asked Bernard to help them determine what was to be done.

He decided in favour of the exile, took him back to Italy and succeeded in getting the Powers to accept him. That success made him more widely known than before, and soon he was going off on new peacemaking expeditions, at the end of one of which he was offered the Archbishopric of Milan. But he declined the offer, and, as always, went back to Clairvaux to immerse himself in meditation and prayer. It was at this time that he wrote his well-known *Sermons on the "Song of Songs."*

That was the period of Clairvaux's great success; for genuine piety, genuine self-denial and genuine enthusiasm are always successful—in the end, if not immediately. Daughter-houses were founded in Germany, Switzerland, Italy, Portugal, and, of course, England.

You know Rievaulx ("Rich Valley")? That was the eleventh daughter-house of Clairvaux, founded in the stormy years of the English-Scottish wars.

You have been to Furness Abbey? That was another of them. So was Fountains Abbey—rather a fine name this, given symbolically; for "thence," says the chronicler, "as from the fountains of the Saviour, very many have drunk waters springing up into eternal life."

With Bernard's peacemaking expeditions were mingled theological disputations; and in the last part of his life he was mixed up with the Second Crusade, which he preached, by commission from the Pope, with the greatest enthusiasm. The chroniclers describe his vigorous spirit as inhabiting a body so frail that it seemed scarcely to be alive. As he passed up and down France and Germany distributing crosses to his recruits for the Holy War, the cities and towns emptied themselves of men as if by magic. "Scarcely," he wrote, "can you find one man to every seven women." Such enthusiasm greeted his preaching that he could meet it only by cutting little crosses out of his very habit. But the Crusade was a military failure, and he died, four years after its close, a saddened man.

Yet in more spheres than one his infectious enthusiasm had accomplished marvels. He had founded no less than one hundred and sixty-three religious houses, all over Europe. Canonized twenty-one years after his death, he was the first of the Cistercian saints. He was a great theologian and a great organizer; had he so wished, he might have been a great statesman. But before everything else he was a great lover of God. As a writer on love, he has been surpassed, perhaps, by only one man: St. Paul; and by him only in one place—that wonderful thirteenth chapter of the first epistle to the Corinthians. Consider, for example, this short extract from the *Sermons on the "Song of Songs"*:

> Love abounds in itself; where love has come, it transfers all other affections into itself and takes them captive. Therefore he who loves loves, and knows naught else. . . .
>
> Love is sufficient to itself; it pleases by itself and for its own sake. It is its own merit, its own reward. Love seeks neither cause nor fruit beyond itself. It is its own fruit. . . .

> I love because I love; I love in order that I may love. . . . I hold in suspicion the love which depends on the hope of acquiring something. Pure love gathers no strength from hope, nor suffers loss through distrust.

There is room for a week of meditation there—it is what St. Francis of Sales used to call a real "spiritual nosegay."

The book of St. Bernard's that we are to glance at now is called, in Latin, *De Diligendo Deo.* It tells of the Christian's love for God, and shows how nothing but love for God, not even love for our dearest on earth, can be wholly satisfying. "My God, my Helper," is its prayer, "I love Thee according to Thy gift, and in my measure, less indeed than is just, but of a truth not less than my power—I, who cannot do as much as I ought, and yet cannot do beyond what I can. When Thou shalt deign to give more, I shall be able to love more, though never in proportion to Thy deserving."

St. Bernard distinguishes four "degrees," or "stages," of love. In the first stage, a man loves only himself, and for his own sake: he is still an "animal and carnal" creature and he has no idea how to love anyone else. Then he attains to a certain degree of love for God; seeing that he "cannot subsist of himself, he begins by faith to seek God and to love Him," but still only for his own sake—for what he can get out of Him, as we should put it—and not for Himself. But, as he gradually learns to know God through reading, meditation, prayer, and obedience, he tastes and sees how gracious He is and so comes to love Him for Himself. "Assuredly," continues St. Bernard, "the abiding in this degree is long; and I know not if the fourth is perfectly attained by any man in this life." At this final stage the man "loves not even himself except for the sake of God."

Then comes a beautiful chapter which gives us, as it were, a pre-view of Heaven, a chapter most dear to many whose hearts are surely fixed where true joys are to be found. What, asks St. Bernard, of souls already set free from the body? Can they have perfect love? No; for though "we believe them to be wholly plunged into that boundless ocean of eternal light and of luminous eternity," they are "not yet entirely changed from themselves."

> Therefore, until death is swallowed up in victory, and the perennial light so invades and takes possession of the boundaries of night on every side that the heavenly glory shines forth even in the bodies, the souls cannot wholly unload themselves and pass over onto God.

But, after the resurrection, God can indeed be loved "supremely and alone"; and then the soul will love not even itself save for His sake, so that He will be "the reward of those that love Him, the eternal reward of those that love eternally."

Take this *Book of the Love of God*, then; read it and re-read it; bathe in its majestic language; go to the Biblical sources of its quotations and rest in them and meditate upon them too. And, having done that, turn to Neale's translation of St. Bernard's lovely hymn and learn from it love's simple eloquence:

Jesu, the hope of souls forlorn!
How good to them for sin that mourn!
To them that seek Thee, O how kind!
But what art Thou to them that find?

No tongue of mortal can express,
No letters write its blessedness:
Alone who hath Thee in his heart
Knows, love of Jesus, what thou art.

I seek for Jesus in repose,
When round my heart its chambers close;
Abroad, and when I shut the door,
I long for Jesus evermore.

BOOKS

EDITIONS

* *The Book of St. Bernard on the Love of God*. Trans. and ed. Edmund G. Gardner. London, n. d. (Latin and English text. This edition, with slight changes, has been followed above.)

Saint Bernard on the Love of God. Trans. T. L. Connolly, S. J. London, 1937. (Includes both *De diligendo Deo* and extracts from *Sermons on the "Song of Songs."*)

Selections from his . . . writings. Trans. E. Grimley. Cambridge, 1910.

STUDIES

Five Centuries of Religion. G. G. Coulton. Vol. I. St. Bernard, his predecessors and successors. Cambridge, 1923.

The Life and Times of Saint Bernard, Abbot of Clairvaux. J. C. Morison. London, 1901.

Saint Bernard of Clairvaux. Watkyn W. Williams. Manchester, 1935.

III

RAMON LULL

The Book of the Lover and the Beloved

III

RAMON LULL

The Book of the Lover and the Beloved

RAMON LULL, a Majorcan missionary who preached the Gospel over half the mediæval world, was born at Palma, the capital of Majorca, about 1232, and stoned to death by Moors in North Africa when he was over eighty. He was a curious combination of the practical man and the visionary. As a boy, he was given a good education and spent his early life in the service of the King of Catalonia and Aragon. He travelled widely with the King, lived a gay life, and, though he was married and had two children, a none too moral one. He is said once to have galloped on horseback into a church in pursuit of one of the ladies whom he coveted, while she was saying her prayers there.[1] Eventually she herself arrested his intrigues. Summoning him to attend her in some secluded place, she uncovered herself and disclosed a breast that was being slowly consumed by a loathsome cancer. "See, Ramon," she cried, "the foulness of this body that has won thy affection! How much better

[1] That story is probably legendary but it is significant that it could ever have been told of him.

hadst thou done to have set thy love on Jesus Christ, of Whom thou mayest have a prize that is eternal!"

But this experience, though it must have shocked him into a more sober mood, was not sufficient to reclaim him. "It was Thy Passion, O Lord," he says himself, "that aroused and awakened Thy servant, when he was . . . dead in mortal sins." One summer evening, when he was sitting in his chamber, composing some amorous verses, he looked up and suddenly saw before him the figure of "our Lord God Jesus Christ hanging upon the Cross." Five times in all did this vision come to him before "the pricking of his conscience told him that he should wholly abandon the world and devote himself to His service."[2]

As he had enough money for his family to live on, he decided to learn more about the Christian religion and then to devote his life to preaching it. In order to be able to preach in Africa, he bought a Moorish slave who taught him Arabic, and, after nine years' preparation, he began his life-work. For nearly forty years he travelled incessantly. He visited France, Germany, Italy, Palestine, Cyprus, Rhodes, Malta, Armenia, Tunis, and no one knows how many other places. Often he was pleading with kings and popes for missionary colleges, preaching campaigns, armed crusades, reforms within the Church, and much more. Now and again he attended Chapters-General of Dominicans and Franciscans with similar motives. For long periods he would be at the Universities, notably the

[2] *A Life of Ramon Lull* (written about 1311), London, 1927, pp. 2, 3.

great University of Paris, lecturing on his *Ars Magna* or disputing with the exponents of the fashionable heresy, Averroism. And all the time he was composing hundreds of books—some in Latin, others in his native Catalan—treatises on theology, philosophy, chivalry, and natural science; religious romances, collections of proverbs, poetry, letters, and a great deal more. One of the most practical things he did was to establish a language school for missionaries, which he hoped would be the forerunner of a great many more. This one was known as Miramar, and he built it on a beautiful site in the north-west of Majorca, overlooking the Mediterranean. It was subsidized by the king, with an annual sum of five hundred golden florins, and thirteen friars were to live in it for the purpose of studying Arabic. Unfortunately, after a few years, the foundation came to an end, though the buildings remained for a long time as a centre of religious instruction and culture.

A great many of Ramon Lull's books are still of interest, for widely varying reasons. The vast *Book of Contemplation*, which must contain about a million words, is an encyclopædia of life in mediæval Catalonia. *The Book of the Gentile and the Three Wise Men* is a picturesque experiment in apologetics. *Felix, or the Book of Marvels* is a fantastic religious romance, part of which, the *Book of the Beasts*, is complete in itself—a charming animal-story after the style of the tale we know as "Reynard the Fox." *Blanquerna* is the imaginary biography of a boy who enters the religious life and eventually becomes Pope—and then lays down his high office in order to devote his last days to contemplation.

Inset in *Blanquerna*, as the *Book of the Beasts* is in *Felix*, is the little work which has made Ramon Lull famous: *The Book of the Lover and the Beloved*. This takes us from the African preachings and the disputations of the Sorbonne to those long night-watches and days of retreat which must always have accompanied them. Or the thoughts which it gives us may first have come to the young convert in the solitude of his early retreats. There is a passage in *Blanquerna,* again, describing the daily life of the hero after he has renounced the papacy and withdrawn from the world, which is generally taken as in essence autobiographical. It may very well be so:

> Blanquerna rose daily at midnight, and opened the windows of his cell, that he might behold the heavens and the stars, and began his prayer as devoutly as he might, to the end that his whole soul should be with God, and his eyes in weeping and tears. When Blanquerna had remained in contemplation and tears for a long time, even to the hours of Matins, he entered the church and rang for Matins, and the deacon came to assist him to say Matins. After dawn he sang Mass. When he had sung Mass, Blanquerna spake certain words of God to the deacon, to the end that he might cause him to love God, and they spake both together of God and of His works, and wept together through the great devotion which they had to the words which they spake. After these words the deacon entered the

garden, and worked in divers manners, and Blanquerna left the church and took recreation in his soul from the work which his body had done, and he looked upon the mountains and the plains that he might have recreation therein.

So soon as Blanquerna felt himself refreshed, he betook himself again straightway to prayer and contemplation, or read in the books of Divine Scripture. . . . After this he slept, to the end that he might the better endure the labours of the night. When he had slept, he washed his hands and his face, and remained alone until it was the hour to ring for Vespers, to the which came the deacon; and when they had ended Vespers they said Compline, and the deacon departed, and Blanquerna entered into consideration of those things which were the most pleasing to him, and might best prepare him to enter upon his prayers.

The book is very short, and, one might think, at first sight, disconnected: it contains three hundred and sixty-five passages of a few lines each, intended for daily meditation. But through them all runs an element of unity derived from three main characters. First, there is the Lover, "the faithful and devout Christian," "longsuffering, patient, humble, fearful, diligent, trustful," who is seeking the Beloved—that is, God—by paths that are long and perilous, wearying his body, casting away his wealth and leaving the joys of this world. But to reach the Beloved is a goal which more than justifies these hardships. For the Beloved, immanent and transcendent, Creator and Redeemer of mankind, who can be sought and found by man, through goodness, beauty, and truth, is "infinite in greatness and power and wisdom and love and perfection."

> Thou, O my Beloved, art so great a Whole, that Thou canst abound and be wholly of each one who gives himself to Thee.

Besides these two sharply drawn characters, there is a third, a rather shadowy, allegorical one—Love. He appears to represent the love of either Lover or Beloved indifferently. On the one hand, he is the Lover's inspiration. He goes apart with him to meditate on the Beloved; when the Lover is forgetful of Him he falls sick, or vanishes and cannot be found. On the other hand, he is a powerful and transcendent personality, endowing the Lover with noble gifts, giving him trials to bear, and "nurturing and directing" his life so that he may be able to vanquish his mortal enemies. A robust character, he is the sworn foe of Indifference and does battle at the side of Truth against Falsehood. He gives himself only to those who desire him, and, in a striking phrase, he "stands between" Lover and Beloved.

> On the right side of Love stands the Beloved, and on the left side is the Lover: and thus he cannot reach the Beloved unless he pass through Love.

The ideal of the book is union between Lover and Beloved, in a sense not too exactly defined. Complete surrender on the part of the Lover ("I would give Thee all of myself that I may have all of Thee, and Thou all of me") leads to a fusion in which "whether they are near or far is all one; for their love mingles as water mingles with wine. They are linked as heat with light, they agree and are united as Essence and Being."

A life like this—a life of an intimacy with God unknown to those who live outside the wall—completely reverses conventional values. How, for example, does the Lover define happiness? As "sorrow borne for Love." What is meant by dishonour? Why, forgetting the Beloved. Who is rich? "He that loves truth." What is loneliness? The companionship of many people. What is companionship? The presence of the Beloved.

> The Lover was all alone, in the shade of a fair tree. Men passed by that place, and asked him why he was alone. And the Lover answered: "I *am* alone, now that I have seen you and heard you; until now, I was in the company of my Beloved."

Those are the general lines of that attractive little book, which some readers have put next to the *Imitation of Christ* as the second greatest devotional book in the world. It is probably indebted to Moslem sources: in his introduction to it Lull refers to "certain men called Sufis," who "have words of love . . . by the exposition whereof the understanding soars aloft, and the will likewise soars, and is increased in devotion." And probably it is this Moslem inspiration which helps to infuse it with poetry, not least with the poetry of nature. Everybody loves the beautiful bird-passages, with the curious enigmatical images:

> The bird sang in the garden of the Beloved. The Lover came, and he said to the bird: "If we understand not one another in speech, we may make ourselves understood by love; for in thy song I see my Beloved before mine eyes."

> "O bird that singest of love, ask thou of my Beloved, Who has taken me to be His servant, wherefore He tortures me with love." The bird replied: "If Love made thee not to bear trials, wherewith couldst thou show thy love for Him?"

But these are only one aspect of Lull's sensitiveness to nature. We watch with him the turbulent stream, the majesty of the lightning, the swift gathering of the waves of the sea, the sunlit clouds shining as brightly as the day-star or the moon, the eclipse in the heavens which brings darkness over all the earth. We are warmed by the splendour of the sun, watch it go down and withdraw its brightness, walk in gardens or fruitful orchards, drink of their cool, clear springs and rest in their grateful shade. We hear the singing of the birds at dawn in garden and forest, but we hear them also as we tramp over hill, valley, and plain, along rough and thorny paths, both long and short, climbing up into the mountain (expressive phrase!), and, from the heights, descending not only to the plains but to the depth of precipices. Not sight alone, but every sense we possess is stirred by this nature-lover and poet. We listen to the breeze stirring the faintly-trembling leaves; we catch the faintly borne perfume of flowers. And whither does this sensitiveness, this keen delight in the visible world, lead us? To the Divine Nature.

And no less beautiful is the poetical reticence and reverence with which Lull refers to the Incarnation and the Passion of our Lord. Here he follows the Franciscan tradition—he was, in fact, a member of the Third Order of St. Francis. The Cross, for example, is referred to as a "Place" where the Beloved hung for the sake of the Lover. The Incarnation is a coming of the Beloved "in the vesture of His Lover." His shedding of His blood is described as "wearing crimson garments," or "new and scarlet robes." But I think the loveliest of the references to the death of Christ, and among the finest of all the three hundred and sixty-five passages, is one of those bird-paragraphs in which, as nowhere else in the book, the Lover represents Christ, and the Beloved, God the Father:

> The birds hymned the dawn, and the Lover, Who is the dawn, awakened. And the birds ended their song, and the Lover died in the dawn for His Beloved.

BOOKS

EDITIONS

* *The Book of the Lover and the Beloved.* Trans. by E. Allison Peers. London, 1923. (New edition, revised and enlarged, 1946.)

STUDIES

Ramon Lull, a Biography, London, 1929, and *Fool of Love.* London, 1946. E. Allison Peers. (The first is a critical, the second a popular biography.)

A Life of Ramon Lull. Written by an unknown hand about 1311. London, 1927.

Raymond Lully. A. E. Waite. London, 1922.

IV

The Imitation of Christ

IV

The Imitation of Christ

With the exception of the Bible, I suppose the *Imitation of Christ* has been read by more people, and is cherished by more people, than any other Christian book in the world. It is said to have been translated from its Latin original into more than fifty languages, and to have gone into six thousand editions. Perhaps before we have gone much farther we shall realize why. But there are two other things that I want to say about it first.

One is that Thomas à Kempis, or whoever its author may have been, was quite clearly writing for people living in the cloister: any number of phrases and passages in it show that. And yet, until you come up against these passages, you never think of such a thing: you read the book, as you would read any modern book of devotion, as if it had been written, not for fifteenth-century monks, but for twentieth-century housewives or business men catching the 8:30 to town. And the other thing about the book is the extraordinary way it grows on you. You begin it quite casually. It doesn't take hold of you with a few arresting opening sentences, or anything like that. But, before you are half-way through, it has become your companion for life. Before long I think the reason for that will be clear too.

Let us begin by looking at the title. *The Imitation of Christ* does not express a fraction of what the book really is. Still less does the title which a sterner age used to give it: *Contemptus mundi*—"Contempt of the world." Both those titles were apparently taken from the heading of the first chapter: "Of the imitation of Christ and the contempt of all the vanities of the world." There are other allusions in the book to the idea of "imitating" Christ, but the dominant idea is, not of imitation, but of closeness, intimacy, communion. I should like to see it renamed *The Book of Friendship with Jesus.* Not only because that is its real subject, but because, as you read it, you seem gradually to come nearer to Christ. The history of what it can do to you is just like the history of a friendship. You know how, in the process of making a friend, you learn, first one thing about him, and then another, so that gradually you find yourself drawing closer to him; and then, twelve months later, you look back and think: "Fancy, a year ago I thought I knew him quite well, when really I hardly knew him at all." Well, if you *live* with the *Imitation of Christ*, that is how it makes you feel about our Lord.

And now let us study the arrangement of the *Imitation.* There are four books, or sections, in it. The fourth is about the Holy Communion—and very much more suitable it is as a guide for self-examination and preparation than a good many modern manuals, besides being profitable for devotion at other times. As this book stands quite by itself, however, I am not going to say anything about it here: I shall confine myself to the other three.

The first book is written for the ordinary, not very ambitious Christian—the sort of person who has to be well shaken up before he makes any sort of progress at all. Watch the author shaking him: "Why wilt thou defer thy good purpose from day to day? Arise and begin this very moment, and say 'Now is the time to be doing, now is the time to be striving, now is the fit time to amend thyself.' Unless thou doest violence to thyself, thou shalt never get the victory over sin." Well, there are plenty of us who can do with being talked to like that—and not only those of us who are Christians. As a matter of fact, there is a good deal in Book I of the *Imitation* which would be accepted by the sort of person who "doesn't hold with religion." That is, if you merely read it on the surface.

But what Book I is really doing is preparing the ground. With consummate tact, and with a devastating knowledge of human nature, the author leads you on to something better. He is trying to root out the weeds in your character, so that when you begin to grow a divine flower-garden, the flowers may not all be choked. He is training you in good habits, so that your well-oiled wheels of progress will run smoothly. He suggests, for example, that you should try to have a few minutes' quiet every day. And then he tells you what to do with it: "In the morning fix thy good purpose; and at night examine thyself what thou hast done." And during the day: "Never be entirely idle, but either be reading, or writing, or praying, or meditating, or trying to do something for the public good."

And so on. Quite useful, you might think, and quite well put, but just a little ordinary, even a little trite. Yes; but here and there we come upon some phrase which thrills us, which sets us on fire, which sends us hurrying on to see what is coming next. Here, for example, in Chapter 20, in the middle of a succession of maxims about the vanity of created things, the thought suddenly bursts into flame:

> Shut thy door upon thee, and call unto thee Jesus, thy Beloved.

For me those words mark the real beginning of the *Imitation*. It never seems quite the same again. And when we get out of Book I, in which the tender and intimate name "Jesus" is hardly used at all, into Book II—"Concerning inward things"—we realize where it is taking us. Now we begin to see the interior life:

> He that knoweth how to live inwardly, and to make small reckoning of things without, neither requireth places nor awaiteth times for performing of religious exercises.
>
> A spiritual man quickly recollecteth, because he never poureth out himself wholly to outward things.

Now, for the first time, we read of the "lover":

> A lover of Jesus and of the truth, and a true inward Christian, and one free from inordinate affections, can freely turn himself unto God and lift himself above himself in spirit.

And now come some of those words which have been a comfort to millions:

> If thou canst not contemplate high and heavenly things, rest thyself in the passion of Christ and dwell willingly on His sacred wounds.
>
> For if thou fly devoutly unto the wounds and precious marks of the Lord Jesus, thou shalt feel great comfort in tribulation: neither wilt thou much care for the slights of men, and wilt easily bear the words of those that reproach thee.

Then, little by little, the author builds up that unsurpassable picture which he elaborates in Book III—of the faithful soul retreating to the upper room, watching for the coming of Jesus, giving admittance to Him alone, closing its ears to the raging clamour of the world, but intent to catch the faintest "pulse of the Divine whisper."

And as we read on, suddenly, unexpectedly, this Jesus begins to speak:

> My son, hear My words. . . . My son, walk thou before Me in truth, and ever seek Me in simplicity of heart. . . . If the truth shall have made thee free, thou shalt be free indeed. . . .

And the faithful soul replies:

O Lord, it is true. According as Thou sayest, so, I beseech Thee, let it be with me; let Thy truth teach me, guard me and preserve me safe to the end.

Book III, entitled "Of inward consolation," is in effect a series of dialogues between Lover and Beloved. Right at the beginning of Book I we had read: "Let all doctors hold their peace; let all creatures be silent before Thee; speak Thou alone unto me." Was the author, then, leading all the time up to those sublime chapters of Book III? Or did they just come to him as he wrote? Or did he even set down the things which had passed between God and his own soul? We cannot say; but, as we read, we are caught up into the heavens, and we talk with one who himself has walked and talked with God.

Now, I think you will see why the *Imitation* grows upon everyone who loves the Lord Jesus in sincerity. And that gradualness with which it leads you into the Divine intimacy is also one of the reasons why it has become so famous. But there are also other reasons; and here, to end with, are one or two of them.

First, like all great Christian books, the *imitation* is rooted in Holy Scripture. True, there is only one chapter on Holy Scripture, and, though every sentence in that chapter is well known, it is a very short one. But you can see that both language and teaching are Biblical through and through.

Secondly, it is intended for simple and humble people. It never despises learning, but it holds up other things as more important:

> What will it avail thee to be engaged in profound reasonings concerning the Trinity if thou be void of humility and art thereby displeasing to the Trinity?
>
> If thou knewest the whole Bible by heart, and the sayings of all the philosophers, what would it profit thee without the love of God, and without grace?
>
> At the Day of Judgment we shall be examined, not on what we have read, but on what we have done.

Thirdly—again like all great Christian books—it is realistic. Never merely eloquent. Never sentimental. It says a great deal about what St. John of the Cross was later to call the "Dark Night of the Soul." Just before the beginning of that wonderful Book III comes one of the most searching pieces of writing in existence—the chapter called "Of the royal way of the holy Cross." It is an iron tonic, that chapter, a magnificent stimulus to the will. The author can be stern, even with his fellow-lovers. None but is the stronger for reading him, for nowhere is he anything but bracing.

Lastly, there is the greatness of the book's language. As a rule, it is brief, direct, forceful:

> He is truly great who hath great love.
>
> Fire trieth iron, and temptation the just man.
>
> Love all for Jesus, but Jesus for Himself.

None of its hard sayings is wrapped up for us. And that is what we all prefer: truth without trimmings:

> We are all frail: but esteem none to be frailer than thyself.
>
> It were better to avoid sin than to escape death.
>
> What are words but words? They fly through the air, but they hurt not the rock.

And yet, interspersed with these concise maxims are rhythmical passages of the greatest beauty, unspoiled even by translation. Let me end with one of the finest of them:

> Grant me, O most sweet and loving Jesus, to rest in Thee above all creatures, above all health and beauty, above all glory and honour, above all power and dignity, above all knowledge and subtlety, above all arts and riches, above all joy and gladness, above all fame and praise, above all sweetness and comfort, above all hope and promise, above all desert and desire:
>
> Above all gifts and benefits that Thou canst give and impart to us, above all mirth and joy that the mind of man can receive and feel:
>
> Finally, above angels and archangels, and above all the heavenly host, above all things visible and invisible, and above all that Thou art not, O my God.

BOOKS

EDITIONS

The Imitation of Christ. There are numerous editions of this book, easily obtainable.

V

JAN VAN RUYSBROECK

The Seven Steps of the Ladder of Spiritual Love

V

JAN VAN RUYSBROECK

The Seven Steps of the Ladder of Spiritual Love

IN the year 1293, when the powers and activities of Ramon Lull were at their height, a child was born at the village of Ruysbroeck, six miles from Brussells, who was destined to become one of the most sublime devotional writers that Christendom has ever known. His family was probably poor, but we know nothing about it—not even its name. Growing into a promising boy, he was given an education by a relative who was a Brussels priest. In his adolescence he went through some kind of religious crisis, about which, again, we know very little, but we do know that it led him to devote his life to communion with God.

For him, as for Ramon Lull's Lover, communion with God meant solitude, and after some time he decided to abandon the active life of the world, and also, instead of entering a monastery, as most contemplatives did, to become a hermit. Not, as Lull would have said, "in the shade of a fair tree," but in the deeper shade of a vast forest, he made his home; for near his native village there happened to be such a forest, in which three religious houses were already established. So here, with two friends, he founded about as small a community as has ever existed. First, these three devout men lived quite alone, unattached to any religious Order. Later, for various reasons, they found it more convenient to join one, so they decided to follow the rule of St. Augustine.

It must have been a wonderful place for that spiritual adventure. "No cloister," a biographer of Ruysbroeck has written, "rivals with the open forest, not only for bringing absolute peace and calm to the disillusioned heart, but for looking up to God with eyes that seek Him beyond the moving tree-tops. A desert is too empty and its barrenness too oppressive; there, man feels driven back upon himself, confined within his own soul by a searching and pitiless sky. The God he there discovers has not a smile for him. The cravings of the flesh, too, instead of being appeased, become intensified in that vast solitude, so void of living beings though peopled with visions. The forest is truly religious: (with) its slender shafts, its vaporous mists . . . , the moaning of the breezes, the never-silent hum of a formidable swarm of tiny lives, and the broad patches of daylight made by the sun, which stands out in the heavens like some glorious rose-window."[1]

There, in that hermitage of Groenendale in the Forest of Soignes, one can imagine Ruysbroeck sending up his mind and heart to Heaven, now struggling with the spiritual obstructions around him, now soaring like an

[1] *Ruysbroeck the Admirable*, p. 103.

eagle in quest of the sun. As he had so few companions, he was obliged, of course, to do some practical work as well, and we read that he gladly took his share in manual labour, and in the most menial of duties, with the rest. "There can be no happiness without work" was a favourite saying of his. As a practical man, however, he seems to have been no great success. The others had even to restrain him from doing his bit in the garden, because he could never recognize a weed when he saw one and was always pulling up the young vegetable plants by mistake. Another difficulty they had with him was that, when he went out for a walk in the forest, he would often be so deeply immersed in contemplation that he lost his way. What a contrast with Ramon Lull, who went about all over Europe, and beyond it! But, as I said, people of the most diverse tastes and habits can live happily "behind that wall."

Unlike Lull, again, who was equally ready to address a crowd of Moors in an African market-place or to dispute with professors of theology in the Sorbonne, Ruysbroeck was not at all reliable as a preacher. After his books had become known, people of all kinds—old and young, rich and poor, clerical and lay—used to come, from great distances and from many countries, to see him and ask him to speak to them. Sometimes the visits were a success, because, when he was inspired, he had a remarkable eloquence. But when he was not inspired he had not the practical man's gift of sitting down and making up something. He simply remained dumb. So it might happen that a distinguished or a learned company would arrive at his retreat, and, when he had come out to address them, he would find himself speechless. There he would stand, in embarrassed silence, and at last he would stammer out: "My sons, I have nothing to say to you," and go away.

Sometimes, on the other hand, the few words he did say would be charged with meaning. One day, in his old age, there came two smart young students from Paris to ask him to give them a motto by which they could direct their lives. Ruysbroeck looked them over, and then turned away with the apparently casual remark: "You are as holy as you want to be." The young men were furious and went off to complain to the other monks that Ruysbroeck had made fun of them. But the other monks realized that there was more in that remark than perhaps appeared on the surface. So they took the students back to him and asked him to explain more clearly what he had said. "Well," queried Ruysbroeck, "is not what I said perfectly true? Your sanctity is conditioned by your will. Examine yourselves, and prove the quality of your will, and in doing so you will have discovered the extent and the worth of your sanctity." The story does not relate if the students were satisfied with this, but it certainly opens up a line of thought which we shall find profitable. Ruysbroeck's brevity must often have been charged with meaning.

As a writer, however, if not as a speaker, Jan van Ruysbroeck was neither dumb nor brief. He used to write, it seems, in the forest, beneath a favourite tree, and, when old age dimmed his sight, he would take out one of his brethren and dictate to him. The titles of his books alone are significant. They speak of the motive which impels men to seek *The Kingdom of God's Lovers*; of the upward journey to that kingdom—*The Seven Steps of the Ladder of Spiritual Love*; of *The Sparkling Stone*, that pearl of great price for which the Lover will sell all he has; of the ideal of union with God, in *The Adornment of the Spiritual Marriage*. And another of his most famous books he wrote near the end of his life (he died at eighty-seven): *The Book of Supreme Truth*.

The *Seven Steps*, which I want to glance at now, is a very small book, describing the contemplative's spiritual journey towards union with God. The "ladder" corresponds to what other writers have called the "mountain" —the steep ascent which all Christians make, in a greater or a lesser degree, and which those who lead a life of prayer can make more efficiently than others. The lower steps we all know. The first is conformity with the will of God, which is the "foundation of all virtue." The second is poverty of spirit, or detachment from things of the world, which gives freedom from every encumbrance: "Whoso is poor of his own will lives free and without care . . . , for, like a wise merchant, he has traded earth for heaven." Next comes purity of soul and body, both these virtues being interpreted in the widest possible terms:

Count no man's friendship too much nor wish to be courted by any; for, though it seems fair, yet it comes to ill and turns to poison. . . . Be wary of yourself and worship Jesus your Bridegroom. Cast out all strange guests from your heart. Break with Him your fast. . . . He shall feed you, teach you, counsel you, for He is your sustenance. He will lead you beyond all created things into His Father's bosom.

The fourth step is humility, with its "four daughter-virtues"—obedience, meekness, patience, and self-denial. With the fifth—"the striving after God's honour in the inner life"—we reach what is sometimes called the "Way of Illumination"; Ruysbroeck terms it the "inner" life, by contrast with the "active" life which has preceded it and the "contemplative" life which is to come. These, in the more usual terminology, are the "Way of Purgation" and the "Life of Union" respectively. This fifth chapter, dealing with both the way of Martha and the way of Mary, is a very beautiful one. Here, for example, is part of the loving soul's prayer:

Thou, Lord, livest in me with Thy graces, and art pleasing to me above all things. I must love Thee, thank Thee and praise Thee, nor can I cease, for this is my eternal life. Thou art my food and drink; the more I eat, the more I hunger; the more I drink, the more I thirst; the more I have, the more do I desire. . . . Thou callest me to be one with Thee, and this is great pain to me, for I would not leave my worship and fall asleep in Thine arms. . . . Could I but attain to unity with God, and yet dwell in my works, I would desire no more. God, Who knowest every need, do with me all that Thou wilt; I give myself into Thy power and stand firm in all affliction.

Ruysbroeck treats these themes, however, as one might expect, poetically rather than practically: one would never take a book of his as a manual of instruction.

Thence we pass to the two finest chapters of all, which describe the sixth and seventh rungs of the ladder—in other words, the life of Union. This, unlike most other writers, Ruybroeck divides into two parts—the "first moment of union," in which God meets the soul, and the soul's "annihilation of God's essence." The former—that is to say, the sixth rung of the ladder—might be thought the highest of all. The state it describes is "the citadel of loving spirits . . . the dwelling-place of God within us. . . . It is eternal, and in it is neither time nor place. . . . In it we are all one, living in God and God in us." But the seventh and final stage is described in language which hardly seems to belong to this life at all. It is as though the visionary had been transported in spirit into the world to come. "We expire," he says, "into the eternal namelessness, wherein we are lost." We experience "a blessedness without measure, in which we are all one, and that same one which is that blessedness itself in its essence; and when at length we contemplate all blessed spirits as in essence drowned and melted and lost in the supersubstantial essence, in a pathless, unknown darkness."

"We are all," he continues, "a single fire of love, which is greater than all that was ever created by God. Each single spirit is a glowing coal which God has lit from the flame of His infinite charity; and all of us are gathered up in one burning and inextinguishable fire with the Father and the Son in the unity of the Holy Spirit, where even the Divine Persons are, as it were, rapt from themselves in the unity of their essence into the bottomless abyss of simple beatitude."

This is language the meaning of which we cannot easily fathom; and it must be allowed that, though Ruysbroeck is undoubtedly one of the sublimest writers in the whole of Christian literature, much of his writing is separated by a great gulf from the experience of the ordinary Christian. Those who live behind the wall will always read him with delight, but often with only partial comprehension. There is an ethereal quality about him which makes one more inclined to credit the legends told of him than many which are current about greater but more practical-minded saints. Reading the last chapter of the *Seven Steps* one finds no difficulty in believing the story of how, one day, Ruysbroeck failed to come back from his woodland retreat, and the brothers, thinking he had lost his way again, went out in search of him. But, when they reached his favourite tree, they found it burning, yet unconsumed, in a flame of light, and beneath it, the visionary, rapt in the contemplation of God.

BOOKS

EDITIONS

* *The Seven Steps of the Ladder of Spiritual Love.* London, 1944.

STUDIES

Ruysbroeck the Admirable. A WAUTIER D'AYGALLIERS. Trans. FRED ROTHWELL. London, 1925.

VI

The Cloud of Unknowing

VI

The Cloud of Unknowing

THIS is a book written, late in the fourteenth century, by an Englishman, about whose identity no one knows anything whatsoever, or can even make much of a guess. He was undoubtedly a scholar, and almost certainly a priest; but, though he seems to have known a good deal about solitude and contemplation, he gives clear indications of having lived in the world. Whatever his state of life, he was a most remarkable writer; for, in days when the language of "religious" books was so apt to be conventional, he is vivid, surprising, picturesque, caustic, and even humorous. His faculty of observation is rivalled by his gifts of expression. He must often have found himself, for example, watching people's curious attitudes and eccentric gestures:

> Some men are so cumbered in nice curious customs in bodily hearing, that when they shall ought hear, they writhe their heads on one side quaintly, and up with the chin: they gape with their mouths as they should hear with their mouth and not with their ears. . . . Some can neither sit still, stand still, nor lie still, unless they be either wagging with their feet or else somewhat doing with their hands. Some row with their arms in time of their speaking, as

> them needed for to swim over a great water. Some be evermore smiling and laughing at every other word that they speak, as they were giggling girls and nice japing jugglers lacking behaviour.

And I wonder how long he spent listening to none too conscientious monks reciting their offices in choir before he thought of that expressive phrase of his, a "long psalter unmindfully mumbled in the teeth."

Here is a man, then, who would undoubtedly have enjoyed the picturesque descriptions and the sparkling humour of his contemporary Goeffrey Chaucer. Yet, whenever he took up his pen, it was to tell us about his life behind the wall. He is writing, he says, not for anybody and everybody—not for "tellers of trifles" and "tattlers of tales," but for those who try to live the interior life and want to know more about it. "I pray thee, for God's love," he exclaims, "that thou let none see this book, unless it be such a one that thou thinkest is like to the book." For, to those who have no experience of what it is about, it will seem mere foolishness.

And what is it about? Well, about the interior life in general, and, in particular, about one phase of it which is very familiar to those who have made some progress. The first step that we all take when we look for the door that leads us behind the wall is desire, yearning—which is prompted by love and produces a resolute determination: "thou mayest learn," in the author's quaint phrase, "to lift up the foot of thy love; and step towards that state and degree of living that is perfect." Dominated by this determination, we then set to work to discipline and purge ourselves of everything that comes between us and the Beloved. We spend time on prayer, on reading the Bible and on meditation. But there comes a point in our progress when these things seem to get us no farther. We have reached a full stop. And worse, there is something separating us from God—we can't imagine what.

We still have the desire—the "naked intent unto God." But there is something between us and God: our author first calls it "darkness" and then a "cloud," a "lacking of knowing"—hence a "cloud of unknowing." How can we penetrate it and reach God? That is the question which this book attempts to answer.

To continue, for the time being, with reading and meditation is useless. "It profiteth little or naught to think on the kindness or the worthiness of God, nor on Our Lady, nor on the saints or angels in heaven, nor yet on the joys in heaven." All these things must be put aside:

> for God's love be wary in this work, and travail not in thy wits nor in thy imagination on nowise: for I tell thee truly, it may not be come to by travail in them, and therefore leave them and work not with them.

In other words, we must leave off thinking about God and concentrate upon Him—"upon the naked Being of Him"— all the fervour of our love, all the force of our will. "By love," says our author, in one of those short, pregnant phrases which it is impossible to forget:

> By love may He be gotten and holden, but by thought never.

We are to "smite," then, "upon that thick cloud of unknowing with a sharp dart of longing love; and go not thence for anything that befalleth." May we pray? you ask. By all means. How, indeed, can we help ourselves? For what else is true prayer but a "devout intent direct unto God"? Pray, then: "meekly press upon Him with prayer, and soon He will help thee." But let your prayer be as simple and earnest as your longing is. Make no attempt to find suitable words or well-rounded phrases. One single word "Fire!" is enough to bring us immediate help from men; one single word—"a little word of one syllable," such as "God" or "love"—will pierce the cloud and reach God.

> Therefore take thou none other words to pray in . . . but such as thou art stirred of God for to take.

Now, this, of course, is not easy. The night is dark and we are far from home: we may not be conscious of any divine companionship. And there are things which get in the way. We are oppressed by the remembrance of our sins, or of sin in general: for the time being we must put it aside. It is good for us to be "meeked"—humbled—but rather "under the wonderful height and the worthiness of God, the which is perfect, than under thine own wretchedness, the which is imperfect." Then, very naturally, those thoughts which we are trying to expel insist upon coming back again. We all know that experience—and no one knew it better than the author of *The Cloud*. He writes of it almost as though it were physical. The thoughts, he says, "rise" and "press continually above thee betwixt thee and that darkness." That is, they prevent us from getting through to God. And, because they are very often good, holy thoughts, we find it very hard to resist them. None the less, we must disregard them, and "look over their shoulders" towards God; nay, we must send them right away; we must spurn them, trample on them, "tread them down." When the thought says: "What seekest thou, and what wouldst thou have?"

> say thou that it is God that thou wouldest have: "Him I covet, Him I seek, and naught but Him." . . . And therefore say, "Go thou down again," and tread him fast down with a stirring of love, although he seem to thee right holy, and seem to thee as if he would help thee to seek Him.

For this process of dispelling thought our nameless author also has an image. Beneath our feet—to adopt his vivid language—we must create a "cloud of forgetting," and, while we forge "stalwartly" upwards through the darkness of the cloud above us, all hindrances to our progress must be engulfed and drowned in the cloud below. Indeed, during this time of crisis, everything must go there—"all the creatures that ever be made"—save God alone. So every "sharp subtle thought," however good in itself, every attempt made by the intellect to invade the territory of the will, must be "put down" and covered "with a thick cloud of forgetting."

> Stalwartly step above them with a fervent stirring of love, and tread them down under thy feet. . . . And if they oft rise, oft put them down; and shortly to say, as oft as they rise, as oft put them down.

This is absolutely essential. The intellect must not be allowed to usurp the place of love: "unless thou bear him down, he will bear thee down." The task is hard: it will cost great effort, great "travail"—"yea, surely! and that a full great travail." But, while we are striving to keep the mind in its place, God, on His side, will be stirring up our love:

> Wherein, then, is this travail, I pray thee? Surely, this travail is all in treading down of the remembrance of all the creatures that ever God made, and in holding of them under the cloud of forgetting named before. In this is all the travail; for this is man's travail, with help of grace. And the other above—that is to say, the stirring of love—that is the work of only God.

The knowledge that He is standing by us, watching us and helping us through the cloud will prove an inspiration:

> Do on then fast; let see how thou bearest thee. Seest thou not how He standeth and abideth thee? For shame! Travail fast but awhile, and thou shalt soon be eased of the greatness and of the hardness of this travail. For although it be hard and straight in the beginning, when thou hast no devotion; nevertheless yet after, when thou hast devotion, it shall be

made full restful and full light unto thee that before was full hard. And thou shalt have either little travail or none, for then will God work sometimes all by Himself.

And that brings us to the last stage which the *Cloud* describes to us: the stage of illumination. For in the spiritual life, as in the life of every day, when you have climbed upwards through the mist and rain, you come out, above the clouds, into a land of sunshine. "Do on thy work," the author exhorts us, "and surely I promise thee He shall not fail in this." Even while we are still in the cloud, He may sometimes "send out a beam of ghostly (*i.e.*, spiritual) light, piercing this cloud of unknowing that is betwixt thee and Him; and shew thee some of His privity, the which man may not, nor cannot speak." And with light comes also heat: "then shalt thou feel thine affection inflamed with the fire of His love, far more than I can tell thee."

That is the main theme of this remarkable book; and I have picked it out with some care because, what with the quaintness of the archaic language, even when this has been slightly modernized, and the author's continual digressions and repetitions, some readers might find the thread that runs through his theme rather hard to unravel. But once you have the thread, you will wander about among the book's seventy-five short chapters most happily and with complete freedom.

And then you will discover a great deal more than has been written here. All kinds of striking phrases will catch hold of you and enrich your spiritual experience. I like the counsel, for example, to avoid "rude strainings" in my love of God, but to love "with a soft and demure behaviour." "Abide courteously and meekly the will of Our Lord," the author goes on, "and snatch not overhastily, as it were a greedy greyhound, hunger thee never so sore." Again, the warnings of Chapter 57 against undue literalness in devotion are appropriate still, as are the counsels of Chapter 59 that a man shall not "strain his imagination upwards bodily in the time of prayer; and that time, place and body, these three should be forgotten." Read, too, Chapters 37 to 39, on ejaculatory prayer, where you will find one of the author's most famous phrases: "That short prayer *pierceth heaven.*"

My only regret about *The Cloud of Unknowing* is that I know so little about its author. None of the writers mentioned in this book would I rather meet in the flesh, not even St. Augustine or St. John of the Cross. And yet I know his book so well that I almost feel I know him too. I can recognize him in a number of other little books written either by him or by his disciples—*The Book of Privy Counselling*, a kind of sequel to *The Cloud*, is the best known of them. I am glad he was an Englishman; and, though there is no room in this little book to write about his compatriots of the Middle Ages—such as Rolle, Hilton, and Julian of Norwich—I think we may be very well content to have him as the representative of the Middle Ages in our country.

BOOKS

EDITIONS

The Cloud of Unknowing:

(i) * Ed. Evelyn Underhill. London, 1912. (Modernized);

(ii) Ed. Dom Justin McCann. London, 1924. (Modernized. Includes also the *Book of Privy Counselling* and *Denis hid divinity*);

(iii) Ed. Phyllis Hodgson. Oxford Press, New York and London, 1944. (A scholarly edition published by the Early English Text Society. Includes also the *Book of Privy Counselling.*)

(iv) Ed. Anon. Abridged. Harper & Bros., New York, 1948.

STUDIES

T. W. Coleman, in *English Mystics of the Fourteenth Century.* London, 1938.

Dom David Knowles, in *The English Mystics*, London 1927, and in "The Excellence of *The Cloud*," *Downside Review*, 1934, LII, 76-92.

VII

ST. IGNATIUS OF LOYOLA

Spiritual Exercises

VII

ST. IGNATIUS OF LOYOLA

Spiritual Exercises

THIS is the story of a young Spanish soldier of the sixteenth century who founded an Order—or, more strictly, a Society—on a military pattern, and wrote a book, as a manual for the use of its officers, which has become one of the best-known religious books in the world.

Iñigo—that was his baptismal name, though later he called himself Ignatius—was born, of good parentage, in a romantic castle near a little Basque village in the highlands of northern Spain. He was the youngest member, and perhaps the liveliest, of a family of thirteen. He never went to school, but was educated by a nobleman, who had him taught riding, fencing, and all kinds of manly games, as well as the irreducible minimum of reading and writing.

At sixteen, he joined the army, and, ten years later, when he was garrisoned at Pamplona, where the army was busy repelling an invasion by the French, he was wounded in the leg by a cannon-ball. Back to the castle he was brought, and there he underwent several painful operations, for his broken leg was set badly and had to be broken again, reset and stretched—all this, of course, without any anæsthetic. It is not surprising to hear that he developed a fever, and lay for weeks—this active young man—a helpless invalid.

After illness came convalescence, and, like every other convalescent, Iñigo kept asking for "something to read." Escapist literature was what he wanted: the sixteenth-century equivalent of the detective story. And that was the novel of chivalry—a long rigmarole of adventures, which to-day would be thought desperately dull, in which peerless knights rescue lovely maidens from dastardly villains, do battle with fierce dragons or baffle the malignant spells of sinister enchanters. Apparently, however, there were no such books in the castle library and the best substitute for an adventure story which they could find him was a Life of Christ written at great length, and in rather a didactic style, by a pious Carthusian.

Lying there, on his bed of sickness, he turned over its pages, and then began to read with greater care, until in his powerful visual imagination that beautiful life stood out with a miraculous clarity and for the first time our Lord became to him a real Person. Exactly what went on in Ignatius' mind we cannot say, but before he was able to limp about again he had determined to devote the rest of his life to Christ's service.

Once recovered, he clinched his determination by making a pilgrimage to the famous shrine of Montserrat in north-eastern Spain. Clad in sackcloth, with a staff in his hand, he made the laborious ascent to the aerie-like site of the old monastery, hung up his sword and dagger as an offering in Our Lady's chapel, and watched the night through, like the hero of one of his novels of chivalry.

But that was only the first step in his new life. The next step was harder. If he was to serve Christ in the Church as he wanted to do, he must get some proper education. So, when he was nearly thirty, he put himself to school, sat on a bench with a herd of little boys and learned his Latin grammar by their side. The work was hard for him, but he made a solemn promise not to miss a single lesson for two years and he begged his master to punish him if he were inattentive.

After two years of school he went to the University of Alcalá de Henares—one of the "modern universities" of Spain, as we should call it to-day—where to find students maturer than the ordinary undergraduate was less unusual. It was at the University that he began to shape his life-work. Gathering together four or five like-minded persons, he went all over the city with them on preaching missions: barefoot, and wearing long grey smocks, the young men became known as "Iñigo's preachers." That was the beginning of the Society (or Company, as Spaniards term it) of Jesus: an army of men vowed to complete poverty and implicit obedience, under a leader of their own choice whom they called a "General."

It was for that army that St. Ignatius wrote his book—

the *Spiritual Exercises*—which differs from all the other books I have spoken of in that it was not written to be *read*, so much as to be *used*. It is a tool, an implement, a text-book for directors of Ignatian retreats—a "teachers' book," not one given to the pupil to browse in, or even put into his hands at all. So it must not be judged as though it were a conventional literary work. We must resist the temptation, for example, to attribute any importance to the fact that parts of it came from other authors. "The entire book was *lived* before being written," remarked a critic of it once. All that St. Ignatius borrowed, he tested and proved, absorbed and transformed, before giving it the form in which we now have it. As many as twenty-five years may have gone to the making of the *Exercises*—to the grafting of a life's experience and a life's devotion upon the writings of others.

The aim of the *Exercises* is a practical one—to train the exercitant in meditation and to guide him in making a choice (or "election," as it is generally called) which will affect his future life: "to prepare and dispose the soul," in St. Ignatius' own words, "to rid itself of all inordinate affections, and, when it has rid itself, to seek and find the Divine will in the disposition of one's life, for one's soul's salvation." The exercises are divided into four periods termed "Weeks." In the First Week the meditations are upon sin, to induce humility and contrition. The Second Week turns on the Kingdom of

Christ, in which we go through the main incidents of His life, as Ignatius must have done on his sick-bed, and prepare to follow Him as our Leader and King—contrasting His service with that of the devil, in the famous meditation on the Two Standards. The Third Week is devoted to the Passion of Christ, and takes us in imagination through the events of the latter part of Holy Week, from the Last Supper to the Burial. In the Fourth Week we think of the Risen Christ, in whose manifestations of Himself "the Divinity, which seemed to hide itself in the Passion, now appears."

These four series of meditations lead up to a beautiful and fruitful "contemplation for attaining love." In what does love consist? "In a mutual communication. The lover gives and communicates to the beloved what he has, or some part of what he has or can give; and even so does the beloved to the lover." Pondering on that theme, the exercitant recalls all the mercies that he has received from God—"how much He has given me of what He has and . . . how He desires to give Himself to me, in so far as He can, according to His Divine ordinance." Then, with a full heart, he resolves in his turn to give all he can:

> Take, Lord, and keep, all my freedom, my memory, my understanding and all my will, whatsoever I have and possess. Thou hast given all these things to me: to Thee, O Lord, I restore them. All are Thine, dispose of them all according to Thy will. Give me Thy love and Thy grace: that is enough for me.

Though they are intended primarily for directors of retreats, the *Spiritual Exercises* can also be studied with profit by the individual. Two of their characteristics in particular will appeal to him.

The first is the use which the book makes of visual aids to meditation. I remarked just now on St. Ignatius' powerful imagination, which, no doubt, was the reason why, as his biographer says, "the sight of a plant, a blade of grass, a leaf, a flower or a fruit . . . would be sufficient to transport him into the seventh heaven." Imagination must have played a vital part in his interior life; he even uses the word "contemplation," not in the normal sense given to it by other devotional writers, but in the peculiar ("Ignatian") sense of "visible meditation." And in the same way the exercitant is continually exhorted to use the "eye of imagination" and to "see the place"—to picture to himself the scene on the mountain where Christ spends the night in prayer, the "synagogues, towns and villages through which Christ Our Lord went preaching," and so on. True, the scenes to be conjured up by the imagination are sometimes of a distinctly mediæval type, as when the picture is to be of Satan, "the chief of all the enemies" of the soul, "seating himself in that great plain of Babylon, as on a lofty throne of fire and smoke, a horrible and frightful figure." But to many people this insistence upon what St. Ignatius calls "visible meditation" is a very inspiring method of training; it proved so, for example, to St. Teresa, who received a great deal of her instruction in prayer from the Society of Jesus and clearly owes a great deal to Ignatian methods.

Secondly, the book has the great merit of being practical. It is meant, not merely to provide a pleasant (or possibly an uncomfortable) hour's occupation, but to *get something done*. The urgency of the call of the true Captain is continually impressed upon us by the constant recurrence of the idea of choice. The very first words of the "contemplation for attaining love" remind us that "love must express itself in deeds rather than in words"; and that is the tone of the entire manual. With its "annotations," its "exercises," its "preambles," "additions," "observations," "considerations," and its constant reference to "rules" and "methods," it will only repel the reader who is not in earnest. In the same way, a Baedeker, with its small print, its diagrams, and its mundane details about railway fares and hotel prices will seem a deadly dull volume to anyone who has no intention of travelling in the country it deals with. But the moment he does decide to go—why, the book simply springs into life. Just so with the *Spiritual Exercises*. Once you are fired with love for God, with the determination to serve Him and with the desire to get to know more of the life behind the wall, where He will be your Companion, you will like no book better than one which you can turn to again and again and find a trusty guide. And such a book is St. Ignatius' *Spiritual Exercises*.

BOOKS

EDITIONS

The Spiritual Exercises:

(i) Ed. JOSEPH RICKABY. London, 1915 (Roman Catholic).
(ii) * Ed. W. H. LONGRIDGE. London, 1919 (Anglican).

STUDIES

Ignatius Loyola. H. D. SEDGWICK. London, 1923.
St. Ignatius Loyola. FRANCIS THOMPSON. London, 1909.
Ignatius Loyola the founder of the Jesuits. PAUL VAN DYKE. London, 1926.
Studies of the Spanish Mystics. Vol. I. E. ALLISON PEERS. London, 1927. Pp. 1-30.

VIII

ST. PETER OF ALCÁNTARA

The Golden Treatise of Mental Prayer

VIII

ST. PETER OF ALCÁNTARA

The Golden Treatise of Mental Prayer

VERY few people nowadays, I am afraid, would be attracted by the life and habits of Pedro Garavito, a Franciscan friar who exchanged his surname for the name of the small Spanish town, near the frontier of Portugal, where he had been born. He followed his Master along the hard and narrow road of mortification and attained extremes of asceticism which to-day seem altogether excessive. Even his contemporaries thought them remarkable: "the world cannot now suffer such perfection," wrote St. Teresa, who knew him well and found him a shrewd counsellor as well as an exemplar of virtue. But he himself took it all very much for granted. "My body and I," he is reported to have explained, "have made a compact together: while I live in this world it is to suffer without intermission, and, when I reach Heaven, I will give it eternal rest."

We have a very trustworthy account of his life of austerity, for it comes from St. Teresa, and she repeated precisely what he himself had told her. For some forty years he had slept every night for no more than an hour and a half, and he invariably slept in a sitting position, with his head resting against a piece of wood driven into the wall. He could not, in fact, have lain down even had he wished, for his cell was ony four and a half feet long. He wore nothing but a habit and mantle of the coarsest serge; and his head and feet were never covered. He fasted for two days out of every three till he was so weak that, in St. Teresa's picturesque phrase, "he seemed to be made of the roots of trees." "He was very old when I first met him," she adds; but it was his asceticism, not his years, that had aged him, for he was only fifty-nine.

This rugged old saint was a silent old saint too—though, remarks St. Teresa (who had a pleasant way with her, and liked to draw people out of themselves), "when he did speak, it was a pleasure to listen to him." He had lived in the cloister as a member of the Discalced (or Barefooted) Reform within the Order of St. Francis, from the age of sixteen. For much of this time he had been a complete solitary, and he was never particularly gregarious, for he always walked with downcast eyes, and he once confessed that, after living in a certain house of his Order for three years, he did not know a single friar by sight.

But if he seldom spoke to his fellows, he was skilled in writing for them. Only one of the "little books on prayer" with which his contemporaries credited him has come down to us, but its wide diffusion has made up for the loss of the rest. Either in its original Spanish or in translation it circulated throughout Europe—in Spain, Portugal, Italy, France, Flanders, Holland, Germany, Poland, England, and Sweden. It was extensively used by Spanish and Portuguese missionaries in China, Japan, and the Indies. Though it was itself to a great extent a summary of a longer work, it was summarized freely for the use of converts and in the Manila archives there are said to be numerous translations of the book or of various summaries of it in nearly all the Philippine dialects.

The title which its author gave it was *Treatise of Prayer and Meditation*, but all the English versions bear another and a longer title which appears to date from 1632, when it was first translated into our language by a Franciscan named Giles Willoughby. He called it *A Golden Treatise of Mental Prayer, with divers spiritual rules and directions, no less profitable than necessary for all sorts of people*. And a book of gold it is: "small in size, but great in quality," as a commissary of the Inquisition wrote of it. Though some of the later chapters are rather more advanced than the rest, it is suitable as a whole for quite general reading. Beginning with a description of the profit to be gained from meditation, it outlines seven meditations, one for each day of the week, and then seven more on the Passion. Next it turns to methods of meditation, and describes what has become known as the Alcantaran method, which has six stages:

1. *Preparation*. Choose a suitable place and posture; "get your imagination under control;" dispose your at-

tention; acknowledge your shortcomings and confess your sins; finally, pray for grace to meditate well.

2. *Reading.* The preparation completed, read carefully over the passage on which you are to meditate, which should not be a long one.

3. *Meditation.* This may be either "intellectual" or "imaginative," according to the nature of the passage. The use of the imagination is very valuable (and St. Peter may have been indebted to St. Ignatius for what he says about it), though it must not be overdone lest it prove too exhausting.

4. *Thanksgiving.* The nature of this will be suggested by the meditation itself. To it should be linked a general thanksgiving—for creation, preservation, and redemption; for the natural faculties of memory, understanding, and will; for the means of grace given us here and the hope of glory hereafter. Say with feeling the Benedicite or the 103rd Psalm.

5. *Oblation.* From thanksgiving arises naturally the desire to offer something to God: first, oneself, one's soul and body, one's deeds, words and thoughts, now and for ever; secondly, the merits of Christ—"the richest and most precious offering we can possibly make to God."

6. *Petition.* Lastly, with all the fervour that comes from thanksgiving and oblation, pray for all the peoples of the world; for the Church; for the State; for sinners; for the poor, the infirm, the distressed; for prisoners and captives; and so on. And finally for yourself.

The first section of the book ends with eight general rules for meditation, which, like nearly all the rest of the book, it is hard to summarize, just because every line has meaning and value. They are the wise counsels of an experienced counsellor, and some of them may surprise those to whom meditation is something new. First of all, for example, we are advised to cultivate a certain flexibility:

> We should never tie ourselves down to one subject so completely that we think it wrong to pass on to some other, if we find in the other more devotion, more pleasure or more profit. For, as the end of them all is devotion, that which is of the greatest service to this end is the best.[1]

Again, we are counselled to "avoid overmuch speculation of the understanding" and to "endeavour to meditate with the affections and sentiments of the will"; not to study as though we were going to give a lecture, for, if we do, we shall be as "dry and undevout and as prompt and ready for every triviality as we were before."

But the most important of these counsels is the Scriptural one that we ought always "to pray and not to faint," persevering even if we fail to experience what St. Peter calls "sweetness of devotion"—or, to speak colloquially, if we don't feel any the better for it. This is something which all writers on the interior life tell us; and they need

[1] In general, for the reader's convenience, I follow Fr. Devas' translation, but I have compared it with the original throughout and occasionally depart from it.

to, so easily are we all inclined to give in. Where St. Peter outstrips most others is in the vividness and the picturesqueness with which he says it. The very glory of the Lord's Majesty, the very lowliness of our own state, account for the "many times that we are kept waiting, pacing up and down like sentries, at the gates of His sacred palace." If, after you have waited for some time, the Lord comes, thank Him for His coming; if you think He is not coming, humble yourself before Him and be content with having done what you could.

> If you have not adored Our Lord with such fervour of devotion as you had wished, it is enough that you have adored Him in spirit and in truth, which is the way that He desires. Believe me, this is certainly the most perilous spot in the journey and the place which tests those who are really devout. If you come well out of this, all the rest will go prosperously.

The second part of the treatise is concerned with devotion in general, detailing, "with our accustomed brevity," various helps and hindrances to it, together with temptations and their remedy. Eight more counsels, as practical as the first, bring the book to a close. I wish there were more space to give to it, but there is this compensation, that the book itself is short, is easily accessible in English and is written in the simplest of language, so that anyone can read it for himself.

It is a remarkable piece of work—a masterpiece of selection and presentation, deceptively simple and full of the wisdom that comes from self-knowledge. It is vivid, direct and forceful, abounding in homely illustrations. How "frail and easily broken," for example, is this life of ours, "since a breeze, the sun, a jug of cold water, or the breath of a sick man suffice to despoil us of it!" How quickly the north wind scatters the clouds, leaving the sky serene and clear! "Even so does true devotion shake off all heaviness, leaving itself unencumbered and ready to do any good thing."

But the characteristic of the *Golden Treatise* that always impresses and surprises me anew whenever I reread it is its sheer beauty. It is irresistibly attractive, not only for its symmetry and clarity of outline, but also, with rare exceptions, for its language and thought. Not that it ever gives soft counsels or imparts smooth doctrines: on the contrary, it is intensely invigorating, and those who take it as their guide must learn to endure hardness and to attain detachment. But one would have expected so stern an ascetic to have written throughout in the tone of the first group of meditations on death and hell, where we find passages quite in the mediæval manner. On the contrary, out of the strong comes forth sweetness. In the pages on the love of God, St. Bernard himself can hardly move us more.

I want to end with a longer quotation than any I have yet made—a quotation attractive for three separate reasons: its own intrinsic loveliness, the fact that no source has been found for it and the interest of comparing it with St. Ignatius' "Contemplation for attaining love." It is a "special prayer for the love of God," coming immediately after the description of the last stage in the act of meditation. Never was precious ointment, never was ardent, white-hot love more generously poured out at the feet of the Master. Let these few extracts give some hint of all that was in the heart of the stern, forbidding old saint as he leaned his head at night against the wooden pillow, walked with downcast eyes through his friary cloister, or sat, while others spoke, tight-lipped and silent:

> . . . Oh, Thou art my sole hope, my sole glory, my sole refuge, my sole joy! . . . O sweetness of my heart! O life of my soul, joyous resting-place of my spirit! O bright and beautiful day of eternity, serene light deep within me! Flowering paradise of my heart! . . .
>
> When shall I be wholly Thine? When shall I cease to be my own? When shall naught but Thyself live in me? When shall I love Thee with the fullest ardour? When shall I be wholly enkindled by the flame of Thy love? . . . When wilt Thou open Thyself to this poor mendicant, and reveal to him Thy most beauteous kingdom, which is within me, which is Thyself, with all Thy riches? . . .
>
> O all ye blessed saints and angels, ye blessed spirits, who burn with the love of your Creator, above all, ye Seraphim who set heaven and earth aglow with your love, forsake not this poor, wretched heart, but purify it . . . from all its sins and enkindle it with the flame of your most ardent love, that it may love the Lord only, seek Him only and in Him only for ever and ever rest and dwell. Amen.

BOOKS

EDITIONS

A Golden Treatise of Mental Prayer. Translations
(1) by G. F. Bullock, ed. G. S. Hollings. London, 1905;
(2) * by Fr. Dominic Devas. London, 1926. (Also includes a translation of Bonilla's *Pax Animae*.) Cf. p. 74, note.

STUDIES

Studies of the Spanish Mystics, Vol. II. E. Allison Peers. The Macmillan Co., New York and London, 1930. pp. 99-120.

In Spanish and French there is a considerable literature on the *Golden Treatise* and its authorship. A bibliography will be found in *Studies*, etc., pp. 414-16.

IX

ST. TERESA OF JESUS

The Interior Castle

IX

ST. TERESA OF JESUS

The Interior Castle

IN THE bare Castilian plateau, in the north of Spain, stands the old walled city of Ávila, a great grey fortress in the middle of a desert, looking from a distance as if it had sprung erect out of the ground in the night like the walls and towers of a fairy-tale.

The ground is hard and barren; the granite buildings are stark and gaunt in their nakedness; but the air is as clear as crystal: you can see for miles. And that picture of Ávila, where St. Teresa of Jesus was born, is extraordinarily like a picture of the Saint's character. She lived in hard, barren times and her aims in life were clear as the Castilian atmosphere, while in purpose and determination she was as strong as flint or granite. She once told her spiritual daughters to "be strong men," and among the verses she wrote were soldiers' songs for a spiritual army. Not at all what one would expect from a Spanish woman in the sixteenth century!

However, we are progressing too quickly. Let us go back to Ávila and imagine ourselves, early one morning, outside those granite walls, watching two little children, a boy and a girl, who are hurrying away from them. They have come through the gate, crossed the river and are making for the deserted open country. Who are they? Little Teresa de Cepeda and her brother Rodrigo. What are they going to do? Oh, they are going to walk all the way to Africa—"the country of the Moors," as people called it—to become martyrs. They didn't know how many hundreds of miles it was; they may not even have known that they would have to cross the sea; but they supposed that if they kept on long enough, "begging their way for the love of God," they would get there. They didn't know what they would have to do to become martyrs either—but it was no great matter, for they had not gone very far when they met one of their numerous uncles, who took them home.

That was St. Teresa's first adventure, and what comes next is by comparison very dull. She was sent to a convent school for young ladies; and, when the time came to make what in those days was the usual choice—convent or marriage—she chose the convent. She went into a Carmelite house in Ávila, and there she lived a quiet and outwardly undistinguished life for a quarter of a century. If she had died before she was fifty we should never have known anything about her. But as a middle-aged woman she became inspired by the idea of reforming her Order: that is to say, of bringing it back to the simpler and severer way of life which it had originally led. So she founded the Order of Discalced Carmelites, which was not unlike St. Peter of Alcántara's Order of Discalced Franciscans, and for the last twenty years of her life she travelled all over Spain, making new foundations.

She became, as you see, a very active, practical woman. She was also a very determined woman. And a very homely woman. In fact, it was quite by accident that she wrote books at all. Woman writers were rare in those days and St. Teresa only took up her pen because her superiors told her to. I expect the reason they told her to was because they were so much struck with the letters she used to write them. There are over four hundred of those letters still in existence, and most revealing documents they are—often on quite trivial topics, but picturesque, vigorous, humorous, vivid, and as full of insight and commonsense as of charm and grace. Oh, yes! Those superiors knew what they were doing when they told Teresa to write!

But *she* didn't think so. She was "stupid" and "ignorant," she said; she had a "rough" and "heavy" style and such a bad memory that she could never remember what she had written last—and apparently it never occurred to her to look back and see! Her method was to scribble at breakneck speed with tremendous intensity, never revising anything, and wishing all the time (she actually tells us this!) that she could be allowed to concentrate on really important things—like spinning.

That method gave us four large books, and a number

of small ones. First, her *Life*: this, in the main, is an account of her spiritual experiences and progress during those hidden years in her Ávilan convent, though embedded in it is an exquisite little treatise which describes the development of the spiritual life under the similitude of the watering of a garden. Then, the *Foundations*, a long series of graphic descriptions of her journeyings during the last twenty years of her life: the atrocious roads, the miserable inns, the intolerable extremes of heat and cold, the struggles with ill-health, and the persecution which she and her fellow-reformers met with from people who had not the slightest desire for her to reform them. A third book, *The Way of Perfection*, was written as a kind of manual for her nuns: full of motherly counsels, it is practical in the highest degree, and yet is interspersed with love-inspired passages of great beauty, some of which form part of an exposition of the Lord's Prayer.

The last substantial book she wrote—and I am inclined to think the greatest, though opinions differ there—is *The Interior Castle*, always known in Spain by its sub-title, *The Mansions*. It was written five years before her death, when she was sixty-two; and, besides containing some of her finest passages, it gathers up the fruits of experience and wisdom, learned first from cloistered contemplation and then from the rough-and-tumble of the world.

The great aim of St. Teresa's life—dearer to her even than the reformation of her Order—was to attain to a "closer walk with God." She believed, as many other great contemplatives have believed, that if you prepared yourself thoroughly by rooting up your faults and imperfections and then strove to get to know God better and better, you could come much nearer to Him than most people think possible in this world; that you could pass, by what was known as the Purgative Way, to a state called Illumination, or, if you were one of the few who could come safely through the terrible spiritual experience sometimes called the Dark Night of the Soul, to another and a still more intimate state known as Union. The *Interior Castle* is really the story of how she herself trod that road and reached that goal; a "Pilgrim's Progress" in which she herself is the pilgrim. But most of it is told in the third person as a kind of allegory—or perhaps one might say painted as a series of pictures.

This is how the book got its title. Teresa's superiors had told her to write something about the life of prayer, based upon her own experiences. While she was thinking what she should write, there suddenly flashed into her mind the picture of a huge circular building—a palace or castle—which must have been made of glass, because she could look right into the centre of it from the outside. Inside the castle were seven sets of rooms, or mansions, in the innermost of which was the King of Glory, illumining and beautifying them all. Let me give the description in her own words:

> I shall . . . think of our soul as of a castle, formed of a single diamond or of a very bright crystal, in which

> there are many rooms, just as in Heaven there are many mansions. . . . Some of these are above, others below, and others on either side; and in the centre, in the midst of them all, is the chiefest of them, where most secret things pass between God and the soul.

The story of *The Interior Castle* is of the pilgrim's progress from the circumference of the castle to the centre. First of all, she finds herself in the dark, cold, outer courtyard, which is infested by toads and poisonous reptiles—that is to say, by all those distracting and mischievous thoughts that *will* keep coming into our minds when we try to say our prayers. She enters the first Mansions, which are called Humility (because we must be humble before we can make any progress at all); and some of the reptiles get in too, though few of them get as far as the second door, which leads to the Mansions of the Practice of Prayer. The third Mansions are those of Meditation; and from then onward the rate of progress becomes very slow.

In the Mansions of Quiet, which come next, the soul becomes more conscious of supernatural help; and from that point most of us will realize that St. Teresa's pilgrim has gone farther than we ever shall. The Mansions of Illumination, of the Dark Night, and of Union are not for us. But that is no reason for our not reading about them. After all, not one person in a million who reads books on the climbing of Mount Everest will try to climb it himself. So don't stop reading *The Interior Castle* when you come to the Fourth Mansions; it's a fine strong air that blows through those last chapters—real mountain air. And it will do us all the good in the world to breathe it.

For one thing which I am sure St. Teresa wanted to make clear is that there really *is* a castle like the one she wrote about. So many people never find it—and never want to: they are quite content to stay in the courtyard among the toads and reptiles. They are very good people—they go to church, keep out of bad company, and do all the right and proper things. Yet as soon as something annoying happens they get all jittery and upset; in fact, they are hardly distinguishable from the people who never go to church at all.

The remedy for that is to get inside the Interior Castle—to get "behind the wall." To try harder and harder, in all sorts of ways, to penetrate as far into the Castle as we can, and leave the reptiles behind. And one of those ways is to strike at the things which try to prevent our getting in, and kill them. It seems obvious when you put it like that; but the trouble is that so few people do put it to themselves like that. Yet that, I think, is what St. Paul meant when he said to the Colossians: "Ye are dead, and your life is hid with Christ in God." And that is what St. Teresa was thinking of in *The Interior Castle* when she developed what is perhaps the loveliest of all her metaphors—the similitude of the silkworm.

She knew nothing about silkworms at first hand, but

someone had told her about their life history. Let me give this in her own words:

> You will have heard of God's wonderful way of making silk, which only He could invent, and how it comes from a seed or egg which is like a little peppercorn. . . . When the warm weather comes, and the mulberry-trees begin to put out leaf, this seed starts to take life; until its food and sustenance are ready, it is as dead. It feeds on the mulberry leaves until it is full-grown, when people put out twigs, upon which, with their tiny mouths, the insects start weaving silk, and make themselves tight little cocoons, in which they bury themselves. Then, finally, the worm, which was large and ugly, comes out of the cocoon a beautiful white butterfly.

Well, in that silkworm she saw the image of the faithful soul, feeding upon the mulberry leaves that grow in the garden of Holy Church and then spinning the silken house in which it must die before it emerges transformed. It would never have grown those white wings and been able to fly if it had not first shut itself off from the world and spun the cocoon. And incidentally it would never have wanted to spin the cocoon if it had not first fed upon the mulberry leaves—that is to say, used the means of grace. And, as St. Teresa thinks over this, she burns with the desire that her spiritual daughters shall profit by her parable:

> To work, then, my daughters! Let us hasten to perform this task and spin this cocoon. Let us renounce our self-love and self-will, and our attachment to earthly things.

> . . . Let the silkworm die, as it does when it has completed the work which it was created to do. Then we shall see God and shall be as completely buried in His greatness as is this little worm in its cocoon.

Do you hear the note of urgency there? St. Teresa continually writes like that. Never, I repeat, is there anything effeminate in her. It will do us all good to read her: it will tense our spiritual muscles and strengthen our purpose. And I am sure it would have pleased her to know that her books still had that effect on people—more than three and a half centuries after her death. Though it would have taken her a long time to get over her surprise that anyone should read her at all—a simple woman with such a "rough" and "heavy" style, who had very little time to write, because she was so busy with her spinning.

BOOKS

EDITIONS

The Complete Works of St. Teresa of Jesus. Trans. and ed. E. Allison Peers. Sheed and Ward, New York, 1946, 3 vols.

Letters of St. Teresa. Trans. Benedictines of Stanbrook. London, 1919-24, 4 vols.

(The translations in the text above are specially made for this book.)

STUDIES

St. Teresa. G. Cunninghame Graham. London, 1907.

Mother of Carmel. E. Allison Peers. Morehouse-Gorham Co., New York, 1946.

Studies of the Spanish Mystics, Vol. I. E. Allison Peers. The Macmillan Co., London, 1927. pp. 133-225.

X

ST. JOHN OF THE CROSS

Songs of the Soul

X

ST. JOHN OF THE CROSS

Songs of the Soul

BECAUSE of the curious way in which their lives were intertwined, St. John of the Cross is generally thought of side by side with St. Teresa. Her writings, as we have seen, touch great heights, and, if we consider with them her achievements as a reformer and her personality, it is probably no exaggeration to say that she was one of the most remarkable women who have ever lived. But, though she continually delights the reader, and sometimes, either by her versatile and flexible mind or by her sheer power, surprises him, she can hardly be compared as a writer with St. John of the Cross, who, besides the same native shrewdness and the same unerring instinct of sanctity, had at his command the fruit of a lifetime's reading, an aptitude for generalization, a technical skill in the presentation of a theme and the marshalling of arguments—in short, the mind and the gifts of a scholar. He, too, had a far wider vision of the entire range of the interior life: his works form nothing less than a contemplative's library, and a library stocked with works of such profundity that few readers can hope to assimilate it fully in a lifetime.

And, with all that, St. John of the Cross was one of Spain's greatest poets, and one of the greatest poets who wrote of the life behind the wall that the world has seen. He wrote so little that for a few pence you can buy all the poems which made him famous, and yet they contain all the essence and magic of poetry, and the poetry-lover can enjoy them to the full, quite independently of their allegorical meaning. His principal prose works take the form of commentaries on three of his own poems, grouped in a little collection entitled "Songs of the Soul," so that if we study this collection we shall be at the very heart of his writing, both in verse and in prose.

But, first of all, let us glance at his life. He was born, in 1542, to a poor family, in a village on the bare Castilian plateau, not far from St. Teresa's Ávila. He became a Carmelite friar and studied at the great University of Salamanca; but in those days the lives of monks, and even of friars, were fairly easy, and John wanted a life of greater self-denial and more time to spend by himself in meditation and prayer. So when, at the age of twenty-five, he met St. Teresa, whose reformed Order, he thought, would give him just what he wanted, he joined her with all the enthusiasm of youth and became the first friar of her Reform.

He began his new life, with two companions, in a poor cottage, so small that they had to use the porch for a church, and live in a loft too low to stand upright in. They slept on the bare floor. Their pillows were stones.

For a window they had a hole in the wall; and in winter, as they knelt there and said Matins, the snow would drift in and cover their habits. Barefoot, they went out every day into the country preaching the Gospel; and soon their sincerity and simple life made them a great many friends, and so led to the foundation of other Reformed monasteries.

But the unreformed friars grew very much disturbed at all this: they were afraid that if it went on a life of poverty might be forced on them all. So they tried to kill the Reform by kidnapping John, imprisoning him in a small dark cell in a monastery at Toledo, flogging and starving him in the hope that he would recant and promising him honour and preferment if he did. But through it all he remained stedfast, and after nine months' imprisonment he escaped, though not before he had written some of the finest of his verses.

He lived for thirteen years after that, till he was forty-nine, for most of the time in the soft and pleasant climate of Andalusia, where he could wander about a southern countryside, and say his prayers, as he delighted to do, under the starry sky. It was in Andalusia, principally in Granada, that he wrote his four great treatises. In his last years he was again faced with jealousy and persecution—this time from ambitious companions within the Reform itself. They deposed him from the position to which his seniority entitled him, so that he died in a kind of disgrace, as a simple friar. But he cared very little about that. He used to tell his friars that if they lived with their eyes fixed on God, nothing else would matter. "Where there is no love," he once said, "put love in and you will get love out." He himself always had plenty for everyone.

For he was, above all, a man of God: that was both the initial and the lasting impression that he made upon everyone. "He was so *good* a man," was St. Teresa's first verdict upon him. "They take him for a saint," she remarked later, "and a saint, in my opinion, he is, and has been all his life."

"It always seemed that his soul was at prayer," wrote a nun who had a happy knack for description. That was as near as she could get to describing what she felt about him. Others, in speaking of his goodness, would use symbols and call him a "flaming torch" and a "white dove." The habit still persists; and a modern poet, Antonio Machado, has apostrophized him, most happily of all, as *espíritu de llama*: "spirit of flame."

And now let us turn to his three great "Songs of the Soul." The first of them is called "Dark Night." It tells about a girl who escaped from her house, much as John had escaped from prison, and journeyed through the darkness, "lit . . . only by heart's inmost fire ablaze," to seek her lover. She attains her goal, and then she sings this song to the darkness:

> O night that led'st me thus!
> O night more winsome than the rising sun!
> O night that madest us,

Lover and lov'd, as one,
Lover transform'd in lov'd, love's journey done!

A much longer poem is the "Spiritual Canticle," packed with rich and daring imagery—a modern "Song of Songs," in which the Bride and the Spouse sing to each other in turn. Incidentally it illustrates the poet's love of the beauties of nature, to which various accounts of his life bear eloquent witness:

My love is as the hills,
The lonely valleys clad with forest-trees,
The rushing, sounding rills,
Strange isles in distant seas,
Lover-like whisperings, murmurs of the breeze . . .

The third of his great poems, "Living Flame of Love," is a wonderful attempt to describe the deepest and most intimate communion with God. He piles image upon image as he strives to express the ineffable, but perhaps the most moving stanza is the last, the rhythm of which conveys so complete an impression of confidence and security:

How tender is the love
Thou wak'nest in my breast
When thou, alone and secretly, art there!
Whispering of things above,
Most glorious and most blest,
How delicate the love thou mak'st me bear!

Besides his "Songs of the Soul," St. John of the Cross wrote some similar verses. A lovely poem, for example, on the Fountain of life, with a haunting refrain, "Although 'tis night," written in the Toledo prison. And a striking allegory of the Crucifixion in the form of a story about a shepherd boy. Here he uses the artless language of popular poetry. The love-inspired shepherd-boy is Christ; His love is the human soul; and the villain that comes between the two is the devil. Listen to the plaintiveness and simplicity of the last two stanzas:

"Woe!" cries the shepherd-boy, "woe be in store
For him that's come between my love and me,
So that she wishes not to know or see
This breast that love has stricken very sore!"

Then climbs he slowly, when much time is o'er,
Into a tree with fair arms wide outspread,
And, clinging to that tree, forthwith is dead,
For lo! his breast was stricken very sore.

In his four great prose treatises, St. John of the Cross built upon these three poems a comprehensive account of the interior life as he knew it in its fullness, the highest stages of which embody sublime experiences of divine intimacy. But he also gives a great deal of excellent advice to those who would follow him on his quest for God, much of which may be laid to heart by every Christian. His knowledge of humanity and understanding of human motives were extraordinary. As his poems suggest, one of his main themes is the twofold "Dark Night" —the Night of Sense, which means briefly the renunciation of all material things that may come between us and God, and the Night of Spirit, an "incomparably more awful" experience, in which it seems to the journeyer, as it once seemed to Christ, that God has forsaken him. It is noteworthy that this great "Doctor of the Church Universal," whose descriptions of the Uncreated Light of Union perhaps surpass any others, should have written with such clarity and force about the Dark Night as well.

But how, you may ask, can this sixteenth-century saint have anything to do with our busy, troubled, agonizing world of to-day? I believe he has everything to do with it and we need to learn a great deal that he can teach us.

First of all, there is the appeal of the man himself. Not for nothing was he, like St. Teresa, born and bred in the luminous, crystal-clear atmosphere of the Castilian plateau. He sees life sharply; calls a spade a spade; rejects pretence, euphemism, and compromise. And everything that he teaches he illustrates in his own character.

Then he restores, to a world which sometimes seems in danger of losing it, the Biblical conception of the overwhelming greatness of Almighty God. He cries, with St. Augustine, "What can any say who speaks of Thee?" He meditates, like Pascal, on "the infinitely great and the infinitely small." He draws us right out of the petty, imperfect existence with which our spirits are too often satisfied. He uplifts our hearts and desires, and yet he abases our pride. And, as we enter those deep caverns, lit by the lamps of the divine attributes, which he describes in his "Living Flame," we are hushed into reverence and awe.

Once we begin to realize something of God's greatness and man's littleness, we begin to understand the necessity for self-stripping and self-purification if we would undertake the quest for Him. The standards of St. John of the Cross are high; his demands are severe; in the comfortable, easy-going nineteenth century, men called his teaching fanatical and repellent, even inhuman. But to-day we know that we shall never get the best things of life by living in an easy-chair. In recent years we have had to fight and struggle and suffer for things which our fathers and grandfathers took for granted; and we know that the prize has more than justified the sacrifice.

Much more so does this prize of which we read in St. John of the Cross; and what he demands of us is merely to be as severe with ourselves as we think the prize merits. He calls us from a hothouse religiosity into a keen, bracing air which is really the very atmosphere of the Gospels. And we can all find inspiration in those invigorating maxims of his, which ring out as clearly as the strokes of a church bell on the frosty air:

Feed not thy spirit on aught beside God.

Look not at the imperfections of others: keep silence, and have continual converse with God.

Love consists not in feeling great things, but in having great detachment and in suffering for the Beloved.

Keep the image of God clearly and simply in thy soul.

Renunciation, single-mindedness, and detachment: in those three words we shall find the secret of true religion, which is ever-giving, unexpecting love.

BOOKS

EDITIONS

* *The Complete Works of St. John of the Cross.* Trans. and ed. by E. ALLISON PEERS. The Macmillan Co., London, 1934-5, 3 vols.

The Poems of St. John of the Cross. Trans. E. ALLISON PEERS. London, 1947.

Songs of the Lover and the Beloved. E. ALLISON PEERS. The Macmillan Co., London, 1931. (Contains the chief poems of St. John of the Cross.)

STUDIES

Spirit of Flame. E. ALLISON PEERS. Morehouse-Gorham Co., New York, 1944.

St. John of the Cross. FR. BRUNO DE JÉSUS-MARIE. London, 1932. (Translated from the French.)

St. John of the Cross. BEDE FROST. Harper & Bros., New York, 1938.

St. John of the Cross. E. ALLISON PEERS. Cambridge, 1932. (Reprinted, with additional material, London, 1946.)

XI

ST. FRANCIS OF SALES

Introduction to the Devout Life

XI

ST. FRANCIS OF SALES

Introduction to the Devout Life

THIS book stands out from all the others we have so far studied, and in a rather curious way. Most of them were originally written for men and women living in the cloister, and the rest are of such a kind that they make a strong appeal to the cloister. But the *Introduction to the Devout Life* is directly and exclusively addressed to people living in the world—it is not even intended to be read by contemplatives at all.

St. Francis of Sales was the eldest son of a well-connected French family. Before his ordination he studied law at Padua and took a doctorate there. When still quite a young priest, he made a name through his sermons—not because they were particularly eloquent, but because they were not. From early childhood he had had a great dislike for any kind of affectation, and especially for ostentatious piety. He grew into a man with a natural tendency toward simplicity and directness; and, when he began to carry that tendency into his preaching, he at once drew attention to himself. For Continental pulpit oratory is always apt to be of a florid kind, and it so chanced that in France of the early seventeenth century that type of preaching was being markedly successful. Yet here was a man who got right down to the hearts of his congregations by talking to them in the simplest and clearest way: there might seem to be nothing unusual in what he said, but it was put in such a way that no one could forget it.

It was natural, then, that when he wrote books they should be of the same kind as his sermons. By the time his *Devout Life* appeared, of course, he was already a famous man. Not very old—forty-one; but he had been a bishop for nine years. As Provost first, and then as Bishop of Geneva, he fought valiantly against Calvinism, and, later in life, he joined a very remarkable woman, St. Jane Chantal, in founding the Order of the Visitation —for "strong souls," as he put it, "with weak bodies." Besides doing this, and writing the *Devout Life* and a very beautiful *Book of the Love of God*, he gave his name to one of the most widely used methods of meditation; so Christian people are very much in his debt.

The *Introduction to the Devout Life* was written for a Madame de Charmoisy, who was the wife of a cousin of his, and, as he wrote to St. Jane Chantal, "a lady all of gold." It is, as it were, the embodiment in book form of a protest against the idea—too common even to-day—that devotion can be found only among the clergy, among people of leisure, and among those who are leading what we call (perhaps rather unfortunately) the "religious life." "It is an error," wrote St. Francis, "nay rather a heresy, to wish to banish the devout life from the army, from the workshop, from the courts of princes, from the households of married folk." Well, no one wants to go so far as to banish it from those places, but the difficulty is to know how to implant it there. We have so many duties, we say, so many obligations, so many engagements—how can we find time for prayer? That is the question which St. Francis tries to answer; but, first of all, he encourages his reader by assuring him, in the most positive tones, that it *is* possible for him to build the wall of his life from the inside. And further, he tells him, he has no need to go off into a corner by himself to do so. It is not even always an advantage to be alone:

> Many have lost perfection in solitude, which, notwithstanding, is so favourable to perfection, and have preserved it amidst the multitude, which seems so little favourable to perfection. . . . Wherever we are, we may and ought to aspire to the perfect life.

So he begins by guiding the soul "from her first desire for the devout life until she be brought to a full resolution to embrace it" and goes on to outline his well-known ("Salesian") method of meditation, which I now want very briefly to describe.

First comes *preparation*, which to people living in the world, amid the bustle and noise of business, is extremely important. Begin, then, he says, by placing yourself in the presence of God, and trying to be conscious of that presence. Think how God is everywhere and in everything; and how, "in a special way," He is within the heart. Use the imagination and try to picture Him at your side. Having done that, ask Him, in the simplest and most natural words, for grace to meditate well. Finally, St. Francis suggests the use of the imagination, in Ignatian fashion, to present to the mind the subject of the meditation: this, however, is not an invariable part of his method.

Secondly comes the *consideration*, or *meditation* itself —that is, the action of the understanding upon the subject proposed. How exactly the meditation is to be made must depend upon circumstances: sometimes we may be able to spend a long time in developing one thought; at other times, it will be more profitable to pass from one thought to another, but always "quite gently and simply," without undue haste.

Thirdly, *resolutions*. The invariable result of a satisfactory meditation will be to stimulate the affections—such as love for God and for one's fellow-men, eagerness to serve them, a yearning for Heaven, zeal for others' salvation, remorse for sin, trust in God's goodness and mercy. These affections must not be allowed to evaporate and be forgotten: it would be better for them never to have existed. They must be "expanded and extended," and, above all, particularized and made definite. Apply to your own life the incident in the Gospel of which you have just read and decide how in your own life you can put into practice the truths which it teaches.

Fourthly, *thanksgiving*, which should never be forgotten; the *offering* to God of the affections and resolutions referred to, in union with the death and merits of Christ; and *prayer* that God will bless our resolutions and give us strength to practise them.

Finally, as a pendant to the meditation, we have a peculiarly Salesian trait—the characteristically picturesque, yet simple and practical, idea of the "spiritual nosegay":

> One should gather a little nosegay of devotion. My meaning is as follows: Those who have been walking in a beautiful garden do not leave it willingly without taking away with them four or five flowers, in order to inhale their perfume and carry them about during the day: even so, when we have considered some mystery in meditation, we should choose one or two or three points . . . in order to remember them throughout the day, and to inhale their perfume spiritually. We should do this in the place where we have made our meditation, either staying where we are, or walking about alone for a little while afterwards.

Then St. Francis goes on to offer some very wise and practical counsels on meditation, occasionally giving them some curious twist of expression which serves to fix them in the mind. There are other places in the book, too, where such counsels can be found: everywhere, in fact, from beginning to end, there are phrases which can be detached from their context and remembered as aphorisms. After spending a period in prayer and meditation, for example, he says, "take care not to give any jolt to your heart, lest you spill the balm": keep silent a little, that is to say, if you can, and return only gradually to what you were doing before. By making a habit of that, one will learn in time to pass from prayer to all sorts of actions. Such advice, of course, is not always practicable for people living busy lives, but no one would have understood that better than St. Francis, though I fancy he would have added that most people can give more time to the transition than they do.

The next section of the *Devout Life* has to do with the virtues—patience, obedience, humility, chastity, and so on—and also treats subjects connected with these, which, in his own day, were highly topical, even if they are not now. There is a good chapter, for example, on friendships—which includes some strictures on flirtations: "abortions, or rather phantoms, of friendship"—and one on dances and other pastimes which the bishop classes as "permissible but dangerous": though "indifferent in themselves," they are apt to lead one into things that are not. An excellent chapter, which it would do most of us good to think about, is one on "society and solitude." We must neither be eager for society, advises St. Francis, nor yet shun it altogether; and, above all, we must practise "solitude of the mind," into which we can enter many times a day, sometimes even in the very midst of our business.

No less admirable, though less characteristic and

original, are the counsels which follow "for combating the more ordinary temptations." The final section, however, on "renewing the soul and confirming her in devotion," is one of the best parts of the book. St. Francis suggests yearly exercises for the renewing of good resolutions, and periodical self-examination as regards our relations with God, with ourselves, and with our fellowmen. Not everybody, it is true, will find that method of self-training of value, but those who do will admire the methodical way in which the instructions are worked out, while we shall all profit by the devotion which inspires them. Everyone, for example, might resolve at certain times—such as after Communion, or before going off to one's daily work—to repeat these simple words: so matter-of-fact, when one comes to look into them; and rightly, for being a good Christian *is* a matter of fact, a matter of the most important fact in history:

> I am no longer my own; whether I live or die, I belong to my Saviour; I have no longer any dominion over myself or mine; my *self* is Jesus; my *mine* is to be His. O world, thou art always thyself, and I have always been myself, but henceforth I will be myself no longer.

Then, having repeated this profession "again and again," we "pass quite gently to our business and affairs," so that our resolutions "may soak into every part of the soul, and penetrate it . . . without straining either the mind or the body."

There is a great deal more that might be added about

this book, but I hope I have said enough to start you reading it. And in that case I think it will not be long before marks begin to appear in the margin of your copy, and underlinings show that you have discovered how useful a guide St. Francis can be to anyone who takes religion seriously.

BOOKS

EDITIONS

* *Introduction to the Devout Life.* Trans. ALLAN ROSS. London, 1937 (4th Impression).

STUDIES

St. Francis de Sales in his letters. By SISTERS OF THE VISITATION. London, 1933.

St. François de Sales. E. K. SANDERS. The Macmillan Co., London, 1928.

XII

JEREMY TAYLOR

Holy Living

XII

JEREMY TAYLOR

Holy Living

"HOLY LIVING." Not a title that one would give to a book to-day. The word "holy" is even more unfashionable than the word "saint," and to describe a man as a saint too often implies something like condescension—if not pity. Most Christians would rather deprecate the suggestion that they were trying to be holy—though, if they are living up to their name by trying to follow Christ, they obviously are. I wonder why it is that we fight shy of the word: perhaps because it was used too freely and carelessly in the past, and because words are like coins in that, when they circulate too freely, they are apt to get badly rubbed. What the words "holy," "holiness," "saint," "saintly" have lost is some of their virility: they are apt to make us think of such passive virtues as resignation and patience. But in Jeremy Taylor's day the word "holy" had a masculine ring: it was the last word that one would ever think of apologizing for.

The author of *Holy Living*, of *Holy Dying*, and of an earlier work, *The Liberty of Prophesying*, which some think finer than either, is the first of three writers belonging to the Church of England with whom I am closing this book. One of the first boys to be educated at a foundation which has since grown famous—the Perse School, Cambridge—he went to Gonville and Caius College, was ordained at the early age of twenty and then passed to Oxford as a Fellow of All Souls, through the patronage of Laud, at that time Chancellor of the University. In the early part of his career he became celebrated as a preacher with a political bent, but he backed the losing side in the Civil War and during the Commonwealth went into eclipse—at one time he was even imprisoned. A year after the Restoration, however, he was made Bishop of the Irish diocese of Down and Connor and administrator of the diocese of Dromore, where, although he lived for only six years after his appointment, he built a cathedral. But he will chiefly be remembered by those books with the twin titles, and it is worthy of record that he published them shortly after the execution of Charles I, whose chaplain he was, during years when he was very much out of favour. It is not the first time that an apparent misfortune has led to the production of a great piece of writing.

For a great book *The Rule and Exercises of Holy Living* undoubtedly is. Great because of its scope, which in this restricted space I cannot even attempt to encompass: examine any one of its chapters—"Of Christian sobriety," "Of Christian justice," "Of Christian religion"

—and observe how widely Taylor throws his net and how vast an experience it encloses. Greater still, perhaps, because of his language: there is no prose work of the period which I read with a deeper satisfaction—and it is worth recalling that it is almost contemporary with the 1662 Book of Common Prayer, whose phraseology, now grand and majestic, now penetratingly keen, has influenced our life and our literature for nearly three hundred years. Again and again one can draw upon Taylor's treasury of prayers, as notable for the symmetry and restraint of their language as for the simplicity and the richness of their thought. Study carefully, for example, phrase by phrase, this prayer for grace.

> Keep me, O Lord, for I am Thine by creation; guide me, for I am Thine by purchase; Thou hast redeemed me by the blood of Thy Son, and loved me with the love of a father, for I am Thy child. . . . Let no riches make me ever forget myself, no poverty ever make me to forget Thee: let no hope or fear, no pleasure or pain, no accident without, no weakness within, hinder or discompose my duty, or turn me from the ways of Thy commandments. O let Thy Spirit dwell with me for ever, and make my soul just and charitable, full of honesty, full of religion, resolute and constant in holy purposes, but inflexible to evil. Make me humble and obedient, peaceable and pious; let me never envy any man's good, nor deserve to be despised myself: and if I be, teach me to bear it with meekness and charity.

Because of the vastness of the range of *Holy Living*, I propose that we look closely at only a very small part of it—the third section of the first, or introductory, chapter. That chapter considers in turn three "instruments of holy living." The first of them, which illustrates Taylor's practical outlook on life, is the careful use of our time. The second, purity of motive. The third, which I have a special reason for bringing to your attention, "the practice of the presence of God."

That, as you probably know, is a famous phrase which was popularized in this country, not by the seventeenth-century Anglican bishop, but by a humble cook who was living in a French monastery at almost exactly the same time. Brother Lawrence, who was just two years older than Jeremy Taylor, had been a footman in an important family, which he left because (according to his own account) he was "a great awkward fellow who broke everything." That may have been due to his being lame, and perhaps for that reason alone his new position was more agreeable to him. But it is because of the account of his interior life which he has left us, not as a book of his own, but in the form of a narrative report of his conversation, that he has achieved the honour of a niche in religious history. His prayer, he reported, "was nothing else but a sense of the presence of God." Every morning, when he went into the kitchen, he began his work with prayer, begging God for grace, while he applied himself to outward things, to continue in His presence. All the time, as he worked, he talked with God, and, at the end of the day, "he examined himself how he had discharged his duty." If he was dissatisfied with the examination, "without being discouraged, he set his mind right again, and continued his exercise of the presence of God as if he had never deviated from it." That is the true life behind the wall. As Herbert put it:

> A servant with this clause
> Makes drudgery divine.

"The time of business," Brother Lawrence was accustomed to say, "does not with me differ from the time of prayer; and in the noise and clutter of my kitchen, while several persons are at the same time calling for different things, I possess God in as great tranquillity as if I were upon my knees at the Blessed Sacrament."

Nowhere does Jeremy Taylor achieve the vividness of that perfect little picture, but, if less arresting, his few pages on the practise of the presence of God are perhaps more suitable and more profitable for us to reflect upon.

We are first to try to realize how "God is wholly in every place," yet "included in no place," "filling heaven and earth with His present power, and with His never absent nature." So "we may imagine God to be as the air and the sea, and we all enclosed in His circle, wrapped up in the lap of His infinite nature. . . . We can no more be removed from the presence of God than from our own being."

Having attempted to bring this home to our imagination, Taylor then appeals to our powers of reason. How, precisely, is God everywhere present? First, by His Essence, which, being infinite, cannot be contained within any limits of place. Then by His power—and here comes a fine passage full of the sonority of Hebrew poetry. Next, by special manifestations of Himself and in holy places. And, of course, in the hearts of His people, through the Holy Spirit: "for God reigns in the hearts of His servants: there is His kingdom."

And what does this mean, asks Taylor, ever practical, when it is translated into the terms of everyday life? Well, the realization that God is everywhere will inspire reverence and fear in us; it will give reality to our prayers; and at the same time it will reveal a new meaning in the things around us.

> In the face of the sun you may see God's beauty; in the fire you may feel His heat warming; in the water, His gentleness to refresh you.

And, above all, it will help us to walk and talk with God. Every experience of life, "every act of rejoicing or of mourning," is, in Taylor's simple but beautiful phrase, "a going to God."

> This was long since by a spiritual person called "a building to God [of] a chapel in our heart . . ." In the midst of the works of your trade you may retire into your chapel, your heart, and converse with God.

There, you see, the theologian and court preacher joins hands with the ex-footman and cook. Though one was learned and the other not, both had experience of the life behind that wall. The bishop goes on to show how the practise of the presence of God affects our attitude, not only to Him, but to our neighbour: almsgiving, "decency of deportment and piety of carriage," kindness, moderation and the like. But continually he comes back to the main issue: the relations between the soul and God. Here is his summary of the life lived in God's presence:

> He walks as in the presence of God that converses with Him in frequent prayer and frequent communion; that runs to Him in all his necessities; that asks counsel of Him in all his doubtings; that opens all his wants to Him; that weeps before Him for his sins; that asks remedy and support for his weakness; that fears Him as a judge, reverences Him as a lord, obeys Him as a father, and loves Him as a patron.

I have not by any means exhausted Jeremy Taylor's treatment of even this small part of his theme—one seldom does exhaust him, so much wisdom does he pack into each of his pages of sober counsel. A chance phrase, for example, catches fire in us as we read it—"if we walk with God in all His ways as He walks with us in all ours . . ." Or a chance quotation, such as this from St. Athanasius, quaintly described as "an old religious person":

> There is one way of overcoming our ghostly enemies: spiritual mirth, and a perpetual bearing of God in our minds.

But it is the Bishop's general picture of the life hid with Christ in God that I want to leave with you. A "frequent prayer and frequent communion"—*perpetual* communion would express the author's sense more exactly—which issues in perfect service:

> Teach me, my God and King,
> In all things Thee to see,
> And what I do in any thing
> To do it as for Thee.

BOOKS

EDITIONS

* *The Rule and Exercises of Holy Living*. Ed. A. R. Waller. London, 1900. 2 vols.

STUDIES

Jeremy Taylor (English Men of Letters). Edmund Gosse. London, 1904.

XIII

HENRY VAUGHAN

The Flint Flashing Fire

XIII

HENRY VAUGHAN

The Flint Flashing Fire

IN PICKING out authors who have written about the interior life—the real life, that is to say, that you can live within your ordinary everyday existence and that no one will see—I have, as I said above, taken men and women as different from each other as possible, so as to make it clear that the life behind the wall is not meant only for the few.

There could hardly be a greater contrast, for example, than between St. Francis of Sales and Brother Lawrence, the courtly, silver-tongued Bishop of Geneva and the ex-footman who broke everything and became a cook, unless perhaps it were the contrast between the two great Carmelite Saints of Spain and the poet Henry Vaughan. They were sixteenth-century Spaniards; he was a seventeenth-century Welshman. They were cloistered saints; he was no saint at all, but a man of the world and a doctor of medicine. They belonged to the Roman obedience; he, to the Anglican. But, as a great Englishman once said, "flame is flame wherever you find it," and all these dissimilar writers were genuinely enkindled at the Divine fire.

Not that Vaughan is all flame by a long way. I like the curious name which he chose for his principal collection of verses: *Silex scintillans*, which I have translated *The Flint flashing fire*. That name fits all he wrote, prose as well as verse, exactly. So much of it is dull and unattractive, like the dingy brown flint-stone. But every now and then you get flashes of pure poetry—and of pure love.

Vaughan stands in the long and distinguished line of English writers on the interior life. He tells us, in the preface to *Silex scintillans*, how much he owed to George Herbert, who had died in 1632, when he, Vaughan, was only a child of ten; and anyone who knows Herbert will see at once, when he reads Vaughan, how often he echoes him. On the other hand, Vaughan's poem "The Retreat" appears to have inspired Wordsworth's more famous "Ode on Intimations of Immortality." Like Wordsworth, Vaughan seems to have come nearest to God when he was in the open air. He has left us some exquisite descriptions of the countryside, often in only a few words:

> . . . One day
> I stole abroad.
> It was high-spring, and all the way
> Primros'd, and hung with shade.[1]

He goes to nature when he is thoughful and sad:

> When to my eyes
> (Whilst deep sleep others catches)

[1] "Regeneration."

Thine host of spies
The stars shine in their watches,
I do survey
Each busy ray,
And how they work and wind,
And wish each beam
My soul doth stream
With the like ardour shin'd;
What emanations,
Quick vibrations
And bright stars are there!
What thin ejections,
Cold affections
And slow motions here![2]

And in his happy moods, as on Christmas morning, he thinks of nature too:

Awake, glad heart! get up and sing:
It is the birthday of thy King.

. . . . .

I would I were some bird, or star,
Flutt'ring in woods, or lifted far
Above this inn
And road of sin!
Then either star, or bird, should be
Shining, or singing, still to Thee.[3]

He can say his prayers best early in the day and out of doors: "Never sleep the sun up: prayer should dawn with the day." "Mornings are mysteries."

[2] "Midnight."
[3] "Christ's Nativity."

> There's not a spring
> Or leaf but hath his morning hymn.[4]

And, once outside, Vaughan uses nature as a ladder by which he may climb to a knowledge of God. Grant (he prays)

> Grant I may so
> Thy steps track here below
> That in these masques and shadows I may see
> Thy sacred way,
> And by those hid ascents climb to that day
> Which breaks from Thee,
> Who art in all things, though invisibly.[5]

Best of all, Vaughan loved the stillness of the night; and he has left us a group of poems about the night and the stars, which, so far as I know, are unsurpassed anywhere. They vary from snatches of mere melody like this:

> God's Saints are shining lights . . .
> . . . (And) these all night,
> Like candles, shed
> Their beams, and light
> Us into bed.[6]

to the sublimest of all Vaughan's poems, the one which begins:

[4] "Rules and lessons."
[5] "I walked the other day . . ."
[6] "Content."

I saw Eternity the other night
Like a great ring of pure and endless light,
All calm, as it was bright,[7]

and to a less known but very striking ode which puts into the language of poetry a truth of which the classical expression is in the pseudo-Dionysius:

There is in God (some say)
A deep but dazzling darkness. . . .[8]

Now if you want to understand, and perhaps to share, Vaughan's interior life, you cannot begin better than by studying carefully "The Night," the poem I have just quoted. As we read his poems, we sense a "busy, restless" man, whose ordinary, outward life was troubled, and often unhappy, but who is continually shutting the door upon himself and calling to him Jesus, his Beloved. Night, he tells us in the poem I have just referred to, is "His knocking time"; it is then that he hears "His still, soft call"; and the last words echo, not only Thomas à Kempis and St. Teresa, but all the great contemplatives:

O for that night, where I in Him
Might live invisible and dim![9]

If you will search in his poems, you can go through the whole gamut of religious experience. He hides nothing from you. There are the days of depression when the

[7] "The World."
[8] "The Night."
[9] *Ibid.*

Beloved seems "slow and cold" and God seems to have forsaken him:

> My sins long since have made Thee strange,
> A very stranger unto me;
> No morning-meetings since this change,
> Nor evening-walks have I with Thee.[10]

There are the days when he prays: "Suffer me not, O my God, to forget Thee in the dark." There are the days when prayer gets him nowhere, and he knows that the fault lies deep within him:

> Oft have I press'd
> Heaven with a lazy breath, but fruitless this
> Pierc'd not. Love only can with quick access
> Unlock the way,
> When all else stray,
> The smoke and exhalations of the breast[11]

There are days clouded by bereavement—and one of those gave birth to a poem which must have brought comfort, and even inspiration, to many thousands from whom some husband, brother, lover has been snatched by death at the height of his powers: I mean the poem which begins with that simple but lovely line:

> They are all gone into the world of light;

and in which, after depicting a radiant vision of his beloved friends—

[10] "Begging."
[11] "The Shower."

I see them walking in an air of glory
Whose light doth trample on my days—

he can apostrophize even the Last Enemy as:

Dear, beauteous death! the jewel of the just,
Shining no where but in the dark;

And, finally, he calls upon his favourite image of starlight to express his glorious confidence, his sure and certain hope of everlasting splendour:

If a star were confin'd into a tomb
Her captive flames must needs burn there;
But when the hand that lock'd her up gives room
She'll shine through all the sphere.

If that is Vaughan on a dark day, how inspiring must he not be when (in his own words) God sends him "sunshine after rain"! We can see very clearly then what the practise of the presence of God did for him. "Lord," is the keynote of his song,

Lord, with what courage and delight
I do each thing
When Thy least breath sustains my wing!
I shine, and move
Like those above,
And (with much gladness
Quitting sadness)
Make me fair days of every night.[12]

Perhaps the finest expression of that spirit is in some lines, entitled "Praise," which I think Vaughan must

[12] "Cheerfulness."

have based upon a well-known poem of Herbert's, though Vaughan goes deeper than Herbert, and never more so than here:

> King of Comforts! King of life!
>   Thou hast cheer'd me,
> And when fears and doubts were rife
>   Thou hast clear'd me!
>
> Not a nook in all my breast
>   But Thou fill'st it;
> Not a thought that breaks my rest
>   But Thou kill'st it.
>
> Wherefore with my utmost strength
>   I will praise Thee,
> And as Thou giv'st line and length
>   I will raise Thee.
>
> Day and night, not once a day,
>   I will bless Thee,
> And my soul in new array
>   I will dress Thee.
>
> Not one minute in the year
>   But I'll mind Thee.
> As my seal and bracelet, here
>   I will bind Thee. . . .

The last poem I shall quote has a title which might have been given to a good many of the others: "Peace." It is peace, in the deepest sense of the word, that Vaughan seeks in his "primros'd walks," in his contemplation of the starlit sky, in his sacred moments of converse with the Beloved. But in these lines—solemn and tranquil, yet charged with vital energy—he is thinking of the peace of Heaven:

My soul, there is a country,
  Far beyond the stars,
Where stands a wingèd sentry
  All skilful in the wars.

There, above noise and danger,
  Sweet peace sits, crown'd with smiles,
And One born in a manger
  Commands the beauteous files.

He is thy gracious friend,
  And (O, my soul, awake!)
Did in pure love descend
  To die here for thy sake.

If thou canst get but thither,
  There grows the flow'r of peace,
The rose that cannot wither,
  Thy fortress and thy ease.

Leave then thy foolish ranges,
  For none can thee secure
But One Who never changes,
  Thy God, thy Life, thy Cure.[13]

[13] "Peace."

A worthy coping-stone to the work of so great a poet, you will say. Yes; but I think the great service done to us by Vaughan is his witness to a country *not* far beyond the stars. "If thou canst get but thither," he tells us, "*there* grows the flower of peace." And that country is not far from any one of us: "The Kingdom of God is within you."

BOOKS

EDITIONS

* *The Works of Henry Vaughan*. Ed. L. C. MARTIN. Oxford, 1914.
Selections in most anthologies, notably in *The Oxford Book of English Mystical Verse*, Oxford, 1917, pp. 56-63.

STUDIES

Four Metaphysical Poets. JOAN BENNETT. Cambridge, 1934.
On the Poems of Henry Vaughan. E. C. BLUNDEN. London, 1927.
Henry Vaughan: A Life and Interpretation. F. E. HUTCHINSON. London, 1946.

XIV

THOMAS TRAHERNE

Poems

XIV

THOMAS TRAHERNE

Poems

IN A STREET bookstall, about fifty years ago, a book collector named William T. Brooke found an anonymous collection of poems, in two manuscript volumes, which seemed to him of quite unusual merit. He bought the manuscripts for a few pence —poetry is never expensive!—and took them to Dr. Grosart, who at that time was preparing an edition of Henry Vaughan, and, on studying the poems, declared that Vaughan was their author and decided to include them in his edition. But before he could complete this he died, his library was sold, and the manuscripts came into the hands of a very remarkable man, Bertram Dobell, a famous bookseller who had started his career while only an errand-boy by purchasing books from the penny trays and had founded his business at the age of twenty-seven with a capital of ten pounds. Dobell was far from satisfied that the poems were the work of Vaughan and before long he had proved that their author was Thomas Traherne, a seventeenth-century clergyman who had published a number of theological and devotional works in prose, but who apparently had never thought his verse worthy of perpetuation.

Comparatively little is known of Traherne's career, which was cut short by his death at about thirty-eight. A little younger than Vaughan, and the son of a poor shoemaker, he appears to have been a native of Herefordshire; he was educated at Hereford Grammar School and Brasenose College, Oxford. After taking his degree, he was ordained, held a living near his birthplace, and for the last seven years of his life was private chaplain to Sir Orlando Bridgman, Lord Keeper of the Seals. So much for his biography; of his personal life we can learn a good deal more from his writings.

From the literary standpoint, with which we are not here chiefly concerned, Traherne's prose is better than his verse—a judgment founded principally on his *Centuries of Meditations*, a collection of short paragraphs (numbered, like those of the *Book of the Lover and the Beloved*) containing religious and moral reflections. The finest passages from that book were surpassed by few of his contemporaries, even in an age when the standard of English prose was so remarkably high. His verse is full of imagination; often it is inspired by genuine lyric emotion; it has vitality, vigour and power; and, unequal though it undoubtedly is, it never descends to an ignominious level. But it has several serious defects. It is restricted in scope and both in theme and in phraseology inclines to monotony. It has weak lines, faulty rhymes, and prosaic expressions. Traherne's finest poems are certainly comparable with Vaughan's; a few of them, perhaps, are even greater. On any general comparison, however, Vaughan is definitely his superior. Where Traherne excels is in his most impassioned moments. "The green trees," he says of a childish experience, in the *Centuries of Meditations*, "transported and ravished me; their sweetness and unusual beauty made my heart to leap and almost mad with ecstasy, they were such strange and wonderful things." Vaughan could never have written that. But Traherne, at the heights of his inspiration, could have written anything. He had (to use a well-known phrase) fallen in love with God; and his love of God shines with untarnished brilliance through his life and writings. Sometimes it makes his poems "almost mad with ecstasy":

> O nectar! O delicious stream!
> O ravishing and only pleasure! Where
> Shall such another theme
> Inspire my tongue with joys, or please mine ear?
> Abridgement of delights
> And queen of sights!
> O mine of rarities! O kingdom wide!
> O more! O cause of all! O glorious Bride!
> O God! O Bride of God! O King!
> O Soul and Crown of every thing![1]

One of the favourite themes of his verse, which he develops most attractively and at some length in his *Cen-*

[1] "Love."

turies of Meditations, is the "divine intuitions" of his childhood. This, as we saw, is a subject which had inspired Vaughan and was later to be embodied in a great poem by Wordsworth. But Traherne treats it more fully than either. In the *Centuries* he pens nothing less than the autobiography of an infancy filled with "pure and virgin apprehensions" and a "divine light" which he can still remember. "By the gift of God," he writes, "they attended me into the world, and by His special favour I remember them till now. Verily they form the greatest gift His wisdom could bestow, for without them all the other gifts had been dead."

> All appeared new and strange at first, inexpressibly rare and delightful and beautiful. I was a little stranger which at my entrance into the world was saluted and surrounded with innumerable joys. My knowledge was Divine; I knew by intuition those things which since my apostacy I collected again by the highest reason. My very ignorance was advantageous. I seemed as one brought into the estate of innocence. All things were spotless and pure and glorious; yea, and infinitely mine and joyful and precious. . . . I saw all in the peace of Eden; heaven and earth did sing my Creator's praises, and could not make more melody to Adam than to me. All time was Eternity, and a perpetual Sabbath. Is it not strange that an infant should be heir of the whole world, and see those mysteries which the books of the learned never unfold?

Those and many similar experiences Traherne put into verse which, though for so long forgotten, has, in the half-century which has passed since its rediscovery, become famous:

How like an angel came I down!
How bright are all things here!
When first among His works I did appear,
O, how their glory me did crown!
The world resembled His eternity,
In which my soul did walk;
And every thing that I did see
Did with me talk.

So begins a poem entitled "Wonder." From several others, and in particular from two, "Eden" and "Innocence," it is hard to refrain from quoting. "Innocence," in simple but vivid language, describes how this child "felt no stain, nor spot of sin"; how his "soul was full of light"; how " 'twas summer in December." And even now, when the shades of the prison-house have fallen upon him,

. . . still it seems me to surround.

Whate'er it is, it is a light
So endless unto me
That I a world of true delight
Did then and to this day do see.[2]

Some of that childish joy in life seems to have overflowed into Traherne's nature poetry. He cannot rival either Vaughan or many other nature-poets, earlier or later, either in accurate observation or in inspired expression. He tended to see nature as a whole; and, as he

[2] "Innocence."

gazed upon it, behold, it was very good. The fields and meadows are a "glorious robe"; "rich and glorious" are "the rivers, meadows, woods and springs"; "the beauty of the day," "golden fields of corn," "shady trees," "the evening dark"—all these form part of the atmosphere in which the poet lives and moves. How easily, he cries,

> How easily doth Nature teach the soul,
> How irresistible is her infusion![3]

But it would never occur to him, as it did to Vaughan, to notice a primrose; to wish himself a bird, or a star; or to listen to the morning hymn of the leaf or the spring. Several times in his poems, it is interesting to note, the emanations of nature blend with the distant sound of bells, and worship in the open air, instead of absolving him (as it does too often in our modern world) from worship in church, leads him straight to it. For, in his quaint phrase,

> . . . churches are a place
> That nearer stand
> Than any part of all the land
> To Heav'n. . . .[4]

But the outstanding passages in Traherne are those in which he reveals something of the deeply rooted interior life which, grown man though he is, he still experiences. "I must become a child again," he exclaims, at the end

[3] "Ease."
[4] "Solitude."

of "Innocence"—that is to say, "I must recapture those divine intuitions and apprehensions of my infancy." Well, our Lord Himself told us that we must become as little children if we would enter the kingdom of Heaven, which is within us. And, unless we have the child's open ear and open heart, we shall never know the Divine Companionship:

> He in our childhood with us walks,
> And with our thoughts mysteriously He talks;
> He often visiteth our minds,
> But cold acceptance in us ever finds:
> We send Him often grieved away;
> Else would He show us all His Kingdom's joy.[5]

In one remarkable poem—written, we must suppose, from the heights of bliss—Traherne describes his sense of the indwelling power and presence of God in language which, as we shall so often find in these books on the interior life, it is impossible for us fully to comprehend:

> An inward Omnipresence here,
> Mysteriously like His within me stands,
> Whose knowledge is a sacred sphere
> That in itself at once includes all lands.
> There is some angel that within me can
> Both talk and move,
> And walk and fly and see and love
> A Man on earth, a man
> Above.[6]

[5] "The Approach."

[6] "An Hymn upon St. Bartholomew's Day."

At the end of this poem he goes farther even than this:

> The soul's a messenger whereby
> Within our inward temple we may be
> Even like the very Deity,
> In all the parts of His Eternity. . . .[7]

We can no more make works like these our own than we can those of Jan van Ruysbroeck and St. John of the Cross. But, if we can look at such unattainable heights only from afar, we shall find pictures also of the lower slopes which are quite within our capacity. There is a beautiful poem, for example, called "Silence," extolling the Way of Mary, and the "quiet, silent person" who pursues it. One of its couplets is often quoted to meet a frequently heard criticism of the life of devotion:

> A man that seemeth idle to the view
> Of others may the greatest business do.

The interior life, the life of the spirit, is the real life, Traherne tells us. "The inward work is the supreme." Such "outward busy acts" as

> Building of churches, giving to the poor, . . .
> Administ'ring of justice, preaching peace

have become necessary only because of man's fall. The "first and only work" of man in the state of innocence is still our chief work:

[7] *Ibid.*

. . . to view
His sacred treasures, to admire, rejoice,
Sing praises with a sweet and heav'nly voice,
See, prize, give hearty thanks within, and love
Which is the high and only work, above
Them all.

Every working day must also be a day of rest—of rest in the soul's "One only" Friend, the "King of Glory," Who will enter it and make it His dwelling.[8]

And then Traherne tells us of the motive force of this life behind the wall—of love, yearning, desire. I have already quoted a few lines from that ecstatic poem called "Love." Read it, and read too a poem written in a soberer mood, with the curious title "Another," if you would know what falling in love with God means. Read, above all, the magnificent poem "Desire," a *Te Deum* of love, in which the poet almost shouts with joy at his discovery of the true heavenly pleasures ("all the rest are toys"!) and, in a stanza the more moving for its unwonted dignity and restraint, praises God for the greatest of His gifts:

For giving me desire
An eager thirst, a burning ardent fire,
A virgin, infant flame,
A love with which into the world I came,
An inward, hidden, heavenly love,
Which in my soul did work and move,
And ever, ever me inflame,
With restless longing, heavenly avarice

[8] "Silence."

That never could be satisfied,
That did incessantly a Paradise
Unknown suggest, and some thing undescried
Discern, and bear me to it; be
Thy Name for ever prais'd by me.[9]

Read Traherne when faith burns low: he will fan the embers into flame; for he is all flame. Read him in those moments of high experience when joy is too deep for expression and seeks in vain for words; for he has the words. And read him, too, when you are tempted, as we all sometimes are, to suppose that the life behind the wall should be one of placid fruition, and that, because we are indescribably restless, we have somehow strayed from the true path. Read him in his restless mood:

No walls confine! Can nothing hold my mind?
Can I no rest nor satisfaction find?
Must I behold eternity
And see
What things above the heavens be?
Will nothing serve the turn
Nor earth, nor seas, nor skies?
Till I what lies
In Time's beginning find;
Must I till then for ever burn?

And find the answer to insatiableness in the all-loving, all-satisfying Being of God:

Sure there's a God (for else there's no delight),
One Infinite.[10]

9 "Desire."
10 "Insatiableness."

BOOKS

EDITIONS

* *The Poetical Works of Thomas Traherne.* Edited by Gladys I. Wade. London, 1932 (3rd ed., enlarged.)

The Oxford Book of English Mystical Verse. Oxford, 1917. pp. 63-82 (Selections from the poems).

STUDIES

Thomas Traherne. Q. Iredale. Oxford, 1935.

Thomas Traherne: A Critical Biography. Gladys I. Wade. Princeton University Press, 1945.

Traherne. An Essay. Gladys E. Willett. Cambridge, 1919.